DISCOVER
SHETLAND'S BIRDS

A photographic guide to Shetland's breeding, wintering and migrant birds.

In memory of Vaila, who discovered seabirds at Sumburgh Head.

DISCOVER
SHETLAND'S BIRDS

A photographic guide to Shetland's breeding, wintering and migrant birds.

Published in Great Britain by
Shetland Heritage Publications,
Garthspool, Lerwick, Shetland ZE1 0NY.

©2015 Shetland Amenity Trust

Printed in Glasgow by J Thomson Colour Printers

Cover and interior design by Alan Laird

Authors Paul Harvey and Rebecca Nason

Foreword

There has been a gap in the market for a readily accessible book that covers birds that people can expect to see in Shetland and I am delighted to introduce this publication which I feel fills this gap.

Paul Harvey is an expert on Shetland birds and his superb and accessible text is both engaging and interesting. This is ideally complemented by

Rebecca Nason's exquisite and beautiful photographs. Birds are notoriously difficult to photograph but Rebecca manages to do this with consummate ease and with a real artistic flair.

I feel that this book will appeal to all ages and audiences and will be an essential purchase for visitors and locals alike.

Jimmy Moncrieff

Acknowledgements

We would like to say a huge thank you to Rory Tallack for editing the whole manuscript. Eileen Brooke-Freeman, Martin Heubeck, Denise Nason, James Mackenzie and Phil Harris read parts, or all, of the text and made valuable comments. Howard Towll kindly drew the schematic diagram illustrating the various feather tracts and structural features used in the identification process. Davy Cooper produced the map showing birding sites in Shetland, Emma Miller liaised with the printers and Jimmy Moncrieff first suggested this book. A big thank you, too, to those whose

observations and research have contr
knowledge of birds, and without whic
written this book.
We would also like to thank the photog
additional images for use in the book ar
to reproduce copyright material. Thank
Fray, David Gifford, Phil Harris, John Lai
Nicolson, Roger Riddington, Richard Sh
Tallack, Brydon Thomason & Nature Pho
Paul Sterry/Roger Tidman for your valuat

Contents

Sumburgh Head lies at the southern tip of mainland Shetland. The iconic lighthouse is managed as a Visitor Centre by Shetland Amenity Trust and the surrounding cliffs are an RSPB Reserve.

Introduction

As an archipelago of over 100 islands situated to the north of the British mainland, Shetland is well placed to provide a summer home for countless seabirds and a diverse assemblage of breeding waders, as well as a haven for tired and disoriented migrants.

Shetland's location means that a rather unique mix of bird species occurs here – one not found anywhere else in the British Isles. Species considered to be rare in many parts of the country are relatively common here, while many common garden birds of mainland Britain are exceptionally rare, or have never been recorded in the islands. The purpose of this book is to introduce the reader to Shetland's breeding birds and its regular visitors. It is intended as an aid to finding and identifying these birds but also considers aspects of their lifestyle and offers some interesting anecdotes. It has not been our intention to produce a definitive identification guide to the birds of Shetland. Over 450 species have been found in the islands but, of these, 250 are not even recorded here on an annual basis. Rather, it concentrates on the 155 species that you are most likely to encounter when out in the countryside or watching from the comfort of a window. An additional 23 scarce or rare visitors to Shetland are given a brief treatment within the main species texts. Finally, a brief guide is given to some of the key birdwatching sites in Shetland.

A flock of Gannets, one of Shetland's top predators, diving for shoaling fish.

Breeding Seabirds

The mixing of warm Atlantic water with that of the cooler North Sea is facilitated by the strong tides that flow around Shetland and its windy climate; island residents can expect a gale on 58 days each year! This mixing brings nutrients into the surface levels of the sea and, as daylight lengthens in spring, tiny phytoplankton use the sun's energy to convert these nutrients into food. As phytoplankton numbers increase, so do the zooplankton that feed on them. This forms the basis of a diverse and highly productive marine food web which sustains, among many other organisms, nearly one million breeding seabirds.

Twenty-two species of seabird breed in Shetland, 18 of them in nationally important numbers. Internationally important colonies at Fair Isle, Foula, Hermaness and Noss support the largest numbers and greatest diversity, and provide a wildlife spectacle that, arguably, compares favourably with anything else on Earth. The smaller colony at Sumburgh Head is more accessible and brings you much closer to the birds themselves – notably the ever-popular Puffin. An evening trip to Mousa offers the unique experience of visiting a Storm Petrel colony in the walls of a broch – a 2,000 year old archaeological monument! Indeed, there are few stretches of Shetland's coastline along which at least a few breeding seabirds cannot be found.

Many of Shetland's seabirds, including Arctic Skua, Kittiwake, Arctic Tern, Guillemot, Razorbill and Puffin, are largely dependent on sandeels (a small, energy-rich fish) during the breeding season. Since the mid-1980s the availability of sandeels in Shetland waters has declined. As a result these species have suffered a series of poor breeding seasons, which has subsequently led to population declines. The most recent research suggests that a warming of Shetland waters by as little as one degree Celsius in the winter

Guillemots nest in dense, noisy colonies, where their highly developed social skills ensure that conflicts are avoided.

Puffin with a beak full of sandeels. Many of Shetland's seabirds seek out this energy rich fish to feed their chicks.

has driven this reduction in food availability. Conversely, some of Shetland's seabirds have managed to maintain, or even increase, their breeding population in the islands. Gannets have the advantage of being able to utilise their long wingspan to forage further afield and are able to take larger fish. Fulmars feed on a wide variety of food items, while Great Skuas have been able to adapt their diet, taking fewer fish and more seabirds, contributing to the decline in the Kittiwake and Arctic Skua populations.

It will be interesting to see how Shetland's seabird populations fare in the future. At present, however, the declines of most species will be apparent only to regular visitors and residents; from May to July our seabird colonies remain a blur of frenetic activity as adults visit the cliffs to take on the challenges of breeding.

Shetland holds over a third of Britain's breeding Red-throated Divers.

Breeding Waders, Divers and Songbirds

Shetland's breeding waders are one of its best kept wildlife secrets. They may attract less attention than seabirds, but a walk across a piece of intact blanket bog or a damp Shetland croft reveals that the density of breeding waders in the islands is now matched by few other places in Britain. Thirteen species of wader breed here and all but two of these are present in nationally important numbers.

The pollen record indicates that scrubby woodland covered much of Shetland until around 5,000 years ago. The climate became cooler and damper at this time, coinciding with the arrival of man. These two factors were responsible for a rapid reduction in woodland cover and the formation of peat, which began to blanket much of the landscape, accruing at a rate of approximately one millimetre each year. Today, blanket bog is a globally important habitat, which stores and sequesters carbon, purifies water

and regulates water flow in periods of heavy rainfall. Although somewhat barren in the winter months, it becomes a hive of activity during the short summer. Rich in invertebrates, it provides food for several species of wader, of which the Dunlin is perhaps the one most closely associated with good quality blanket bog. The abundance of lochans (small pools) it supports provides nesting sites for Red-throated Divers.

Much of Shetland's bog has deteriorated as a result of extensive, historical peat-cutting, accentuated in

Cottongrass grows in acidic, wet places and is a major component of Shetland's blanket bogs.

9

Traditional crofting, with its diverse mix of animals and crops, and use of organic fertilisers, provided a range of habitats for birds.

places by over-grazing. Stock numbers have been reduced in recent years through support from agri-environment schemes, and some areas are showing signs of recovery. The Government is now offering incentives to restore areas of blanket bog.

Due to Shetland's remote location, geology and climate, agricultural intensification has not proceeded at anything like the pace that it has over much of Britain and, as a result, the islands' population of some typical farmland species, such as Lapwing, Skylark, Starling and Twite, are still relatively healthy. Traditional crofting, with its mix of pasture and arable, and sheep and cattle, is largely a thing of the past, however. Sheep grazing has become the predominant land use and there are signs that some of our waders, notably Lapwing and Redshank, are now in decline. Several songbird species ceased to breed here in the late 20th century and Twite numbers have declined. Careful targeting of public subsidy will be required in the future if Shetland is to maintain a healthy and diverse population of breeding farmland birds.

Finally, we should mention two very special wader species for which Shetland supports the majority of the British population: Whimbrel and Red-necked Phalarope. The stronghold of the Whimbrel used to be the serpentine heaths of Unst and Fetlar, but for reasons which are not altogether clear, it has undergone a rapid decline there. For the moment, however, the population in parts of mainland Shetland is holding up. The RSPB continues to work hard to secure a future for the Red-necked Phalarope in the islands through targeted management work at key breeding sites.

Over 95% of Britain's Whimbrel breed in Shetland.

The splendid, but very rare, King Eider can be found among flocks of its more common cousin most winters.

Wintering Birds

Shetland winters are long, dark and generally wet and windy. Local birdwatchers focus much of their effort on finding rare gulls, venturing further afield to count wildfowl, grebes and divers in sheltered bays, voes and sounds, when the wind abates. Slavonian Grebes and Great Northern Divers are easier to locate in calm conditions, and Red-breasted Mergansers feed energetically in the shallows. In late winter, Eiders, Long-tailed Ducks and Goldeneyes start their noisy courtship display. All of these species winter in Shetland in nationally important numbers. Freshwater wildfowl are of less importance in a national context, but good numbers of Wigeon and Teal occur, along with a few Whooper Swans. Purple Sandpipers occupy low rocky coastlines and Turnstones often feed on short, damp grassland. Both of these waders are present in Shetland in nationally significant numbers in winter.

Long-tailed Ducks winter in Shetland in nationally important numbers.

The Cape May Warbler breeds in North America. This individual found on Unst in October 2013 was only the second seen in Britain.

Migrants

In recent years, Shetland has become something of a Mecca for birdwatchers in autumn. This is because the islands have developed an unparalleled reputation for attracting a host of extreme vagrants from Siberia and North America. Such birds are often thousands of miles away from their intended winter destination – Southeast Asia, in the case of many of those from Siberia, and Central or South America for those originating from North America. The precise mechanism for this vagrancy remains unconfirmed. Some North American migrants fly out over the Atlantic on their way southwards to the Caribbean or Central America. If these encounter depressions (cyclones) tracking rapidly eastwards, they can get caught up in strong westerly winds, bringing them across the Atlantic to Europe.

A different mechanism might be operating for those from Siberia. These are often termed reverse migrants, the theory being that young birds possess a faulty internal compass and, rather than migrating towards their wintering grounds, they migrate in the opposite direction; Shetland is thus well placed to receive them. Look at a globe, rather than a flat map, and this will make more sense.

Of more relevance to this book, however, are the common and scarce migrants that turn up in Shetland in reasonable numbers every year. These species make regular seasonal movements; in spring they head north to take advantage of the rich bounty of food available during the northern summer, but in autumn they head back south to avoid the hardships of a northern winter. These migrants can be divided broadly into two groups. The first of these comprises species that breed to the north-west of Shetland, in Faroe or Iceland, or perhaps Greenland. This includes Whooper Swan, Greylag and Pink-footed Goose, several duck and wader species, Redwing, Wheatear, White Wagtail, Meadow Pipit and

The Siberian Rubythroat breeds in Siberia and this individual, found at Levenwick in October 2014, was the highlight of the year for many visiting birdwatchers. Nine of the 11 British records have been in Shetland.

Snow Bunting. Many of these intend to use the islands as a migratory stop-over at which they can refuel before heading further south to their winter quarters. Some of the larger species, notably geese, may just use the islands as a navigational tool to guide them on their way south.

The second group involves the vast majority of species and these arrive in Shetland largely by accident. Most of these are birds moving between their summer breeding grounds in Scandinavia and their winter quarters in south-west Europe, the Mediterranean or Africa. As they head across the North Sea or Baltic, they may run into strong winds from an eastern quarter, sometimes accompanied by poor visibility and/or rain. As a result, they drift across the North Sea, or get completely disoriented, and may end up in Shetland. Large arrivals (falls) occur when significant numbers of birds get caught out in this way. If Shetland were not here, it is quite possible that many of these birds would eventually

be lost at sea. The number of migrants reaching Shetland is much greater in autumn than in spring. This is for two reasons: there is a far bigger pool of birds in autumn after the breeding season, and many of the inexperienced juveniles will commence migration even in adverse weather. Come spring, the pool of birds will be much smaller, following winter mortality of many juveniles, and those birds that do remain are far more experienced at migrating. It should come as no surprise, then, that the majority of migrants that reach Shetland in autumn are young birds.

In addition, there are two other mechanisms that are likely to result in migrants reaching Shetland: the first, which we have already dealt with, is reverse migration, which may explain why some species that breed in central Europe (e.g. Barred Warbler) or western Asia (e.g. Yellow-browed Warbler) turn up in Shetland in surprisingly large numbers every autumn; the other is spring overshooting. This theory, for

Whooper Swans from Iceland arrive in Shetland in October. Most remain here for just a few days to feed up before heading further south to mainland Scotland for the winter.

which there is considerable circumstantial evidence, argues that in fine, anticyclonic spring weather, some migrants travel further north, or north-west, than they had intended to, thus overshooting their normal breeding grounds. Such overshooting could also be deliberate, however; migrants that are unable to secure a breeding territory within their normal range may head further north in order to try and obtain one. These individuals are most likely to be young males.

In autumn birdwatchers hope for south-easterly winds as these usually bring significant arrivals of migrants to the islands.

The Subalpine Warbler is a regular spring overshoot to Shetland. This individual, found at Exnaboe in April 2014, should have stopped in south-east Europe.

One other group of birds that we have yet to consider is irruptive species. These are not migrants in the normal sense of the word as their movements are not regular and often do not involve a return leg. Most irruptive species that occur in Shetland originate from the forests of Scandinavia and further east. They usually occur here when a shortage of food in the breeding area coincides with high population levels. Birds, mostly less experienced juveniles, disperse to the south and west to look for food. Great Spotted Woodpeckers, Waxwings and several finches and tits are typical irruptive species. By whatever means they arrive, the excitement of looking for migrants in bushes or on a coastal headland is a real passion for many birdwatchers and a large fall of migrants, albeit a rare occurrence, will remain in the memory for a long time.

Blue Tits are very rare in Shetland and in many years none are recorded. They are, however, prone to occasional irruptions when they provide a welcome surprise for local birdwatchers. The three largest irruptions on record were in 1988, 2012 and 2014, when over 40 were recorded in the islands. Interestingly these visitors from the continent are not as familiar with garden feeders as their British counterparts and often ignore them.

How to use this book

The aim of the book is to help the reader identify the vast majority of bird species that he or she will find in Shetland. The 155 species texts are, for the most part, given in systematic order, but we have made a few exceptions to accommodate similar species side by side, to assist identification. Additional rarer species are highlighted in oval insets.

The names follow those used most commonly by local birdwatchers. The Shetland name(s) is given in brackets where this is still used or has been used until relatively recently. Scientific names can be found in the checklist on page 202-205.

A species name given in red indicates that Shetland holds a nationally important breeding or wintering population, defined as greater than 1% of the UK population.

Time of the year when most likely to be seen. The darker colour depicts the period when the species is most common, the paler colour when it is less common

Favoured habitat(s) and location(s)

Status in Shetland

Key identification features

Additional rarer species illustrated in oval insets

Explanation of terms used in status section

Description	Breeding status	Non-breeding Status
Very rare	Less than annual	
Rare	1-10 pairs	annual, but < 20 a year
Scarce	11-100 pairs	usually 21 - 200 a year
Common	100-10,000 pairs	usually 200-10,000 a year
Abundant	10,000+ pairs	greater than 10,000 a year

Identifying your bird

The illustration shows the location of all the feather tracts and structural features referred to in the species accounts. When faced with an unknown bird, concentrate on its size, the shape and length of its bill, the leg colour, and any striking plumage features. Both its behaviour and the habitat it is using may also help. A photograph or annotated sketch, may help confirm the identification.

It is, of course, possible that you may encounter one of Shetland's rarer visitors, which is not illustrated in this book. A full checklist of the species that have occurred in Shetland up until early 2015 is given on pages 202-205. This will enable you to consider other possible species. If you think you might have seen a more unusual species, we recommend you consult *The Collins Bird Guide* which, in our view is the best identification book available. More details of the status of Shetland's birds can be found in *The Birds of Shetland*, published by Helm (A & C Black).

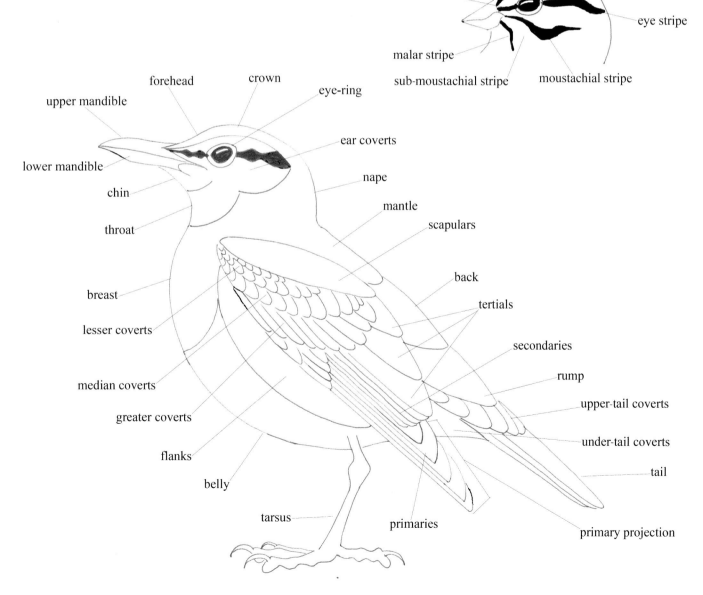

J F M A M J J A S O N D

WHEN TO SEE

WHERE TO SEE

Flocks can usually be found on the Loch of Benston and Loch of Spiggie in autumn and winter.

Mute Swan

First bred in 1992 and a small population is now established.

Shetland's two common swan species are best identified by their bill colour. The Mute Swan has an orange and black bill, the Whooper a yellow and black bill. Juveniles of both species have grey bills but Mute Swans have a dirtier, patchy, brown plumage while Whoopers are a smoother, more uniform grey.

Several attempts were made to introduce this species to Shetland in the early 1900s. A small population did become established but they were shot for food by men returning from World War I. In adults, the sexes can be told apart by the size of the black knob at the base of the bill, which swells up in the male during the breeding season. Despite their name, Mute Swans can be quite noisy especially during courtship, making various snorting or grunting calls.

| J | F | M | A | M | J | J | A | S | O | N | D |

WHEN TO SEE

WHERE TO SEE

Easter Loch on Unst, and the Loch of Spiggie are favoured sites on migration but small numbers can be found at many freshwater lochs.

Whooper Swan

Common migrant especially in October and November, with fewer in winter. A few pairs have bred since 1994.

As well as differences in bill pattern, our two common swan species show subtle differences in shape. The Whooper Swan has a straighter neck and a shorter, less pointed tail than the Mute Swan.

Nearly all of Britain's breeding Whooper Swans are found in Shetland. These are derived from Icelandic stock. Males can be extremely aggressive during the breeding season and often attack anything swan sized and white, including sheep. The bill pattern of each adult is unique, allowing them to be identified individually. Look for family parties; the young usually remain with the adults until the following spring. As with other swan and goose species, pairs will often remain together for life.

WHERE TO SEE

Large flocks occur anywhere but are regular in the south mainland. Grounded migrants and wintering birds favour improved grassland. Look carefully among flocks of Greylag Geese.

Pink-footed Goose

Large flocks pass through in September and October, smaller numbers in spring. A few remain for the winter.

The Pink-footed Goose differs from the Greylag in its smaller size, shorter and distinctly darker neck, greyer cast to the back and mantle, and its smaller bill, which is pink, rather than orange, and usually has some black on it. In flight it shows a pale grey forewing, but this does not contrast as much as the strikingly pale forewing of Greylag. The underwing is also darker than in Greylag. The 'wink-wink' call when given is distinctive.

Restricted as breeding birds to Iceland, Greenland and Svalbard, the population has increased massively since the second half of the 20th century. Many spend the winter in Britain, where numbers have increased from fewer than 50,000 in the 1950s to almost 350,000! Migrant flocks fly in a V formation, with each bird's flaps synchronised to catch the preceding bird's updraft, so saving energy. Individuals take it in turns to lead the flock – the most energy-demanding position.

*The rarer **Bean Goose** (inset) shares the Pink-foot's darker neck, but has an orange and black bill, orange legs and striking white fringes to the tertials.*

J F M A M J J A S O N D

WHEN TO SEE

WHERE TO SEE

*The most common goose
in the islands,
can be encountered
anywhere.*

Greylag Goose *(Grey Gös)*

Common migrant and winter visitor. First bred in the mid-1980s but now a common and widespread breeder.

A large, grey goose with pink legs and a large orange bill, which may occasionally show some narrow white feathering around its base. Large and bulky in flight, with broad wings, pinched-in look to neck, and striking pale forewing and underwing. Their loud honking call resembles that of farmyard geese.

*The **White-fronted Goose** (inset) is a scarce visitor but adults are easily identified by the broad white blaze surrounding the base of the bill and the dark barring on the underparts.*

The improvement of agricultural land and reseeding of hills, combined with moorland and large freshwater lochs, created an ideal habitat for Greylags in Shetland. As the migrant population increased some bred here rather than returning to spend the summer in Iceland. The population now numbers ca. 1,000 pairs. Greylags prefer to graze the growing shoots of improved grass but have to nibble constantly to get enough nutrition. As they graze the grass is quickly processed and passed through the gut so that they are not too heavy to take off. The Greylag is the ancestor of many varieties of the domestic goose.

Barnacle Goose

Common migrant, mainly in September and October. A few sometimes remain in winter.

This medium-sized goose is distinctive with an almost completely white face and black neck. There is a neat cut-off between the black neck and the strongly-contrasting white underparts. The grey back is neatly barred black and white.

*The larger **Canada Goose** (inset), a rare visitor to Shetland, is superficially similar, but with a brownish body and a white patch that is restricted to the side of the face.*

It was once believed that Barnacle Geese developed from Goose Barnacles, hence the similar English and scientific names. The geese were thought to be born from driftwood, feed on the sap of the wood, and then fall off into the water or fly away. This explained their absence in summer. Now we know that they fly north for the summer where some breed on cliff faces to avoid predators. The subsequent jump made by the small goslings can be perilous.

Brent Goose

Scarce migrant and winter visitor.

A small goose, not much larger than a Mallard. The head and neck are black, with a white half-collar on the neck. The body is greyish-brown, contrasting with a white rear end. Note the differences in the underparts between the pale-bellied bird (above) and the dark-bellied individual (below).

Colour ringing can help to reveal where birds breed and spend the winter, and which sites are important for them on migration. Two individuals (one above) from the Canadian High Arctic occurred in Shetland in spring 2015.

WHERE TO SEE

Favours intertidal areas and coastal pools but will also join other geese on short grass.

Like many species of goose, the Brent has several populations (races) that both breed and winter in different areas. This means there is little gene flow between them and each population has, therefore, evolved to look subtly different: the dark-bellied race breeds in the Siberian Arctic; the pale-bellied form breeds in eastern Arctic Canada, Greenland and Spitsbergen; and the Black Brant breeds in western Arctic Canada, Alaska and far-eastern Siberia. The Black Brant has yet to occur in Shetland, although it is an annual visitor to Britain, but the other two races are regular here.

J F M A M J J A S O N D

WHEN TO SEE

WHERE TO SEE

The Pool of Virkie is a favoured haunt, with Spiggie, Hillwell and Boddam also regular sites.

Shelduck

Rare breeding summer visitor and migrant.

Size of a small goose. Adults unmistakable with their largely white plumage, dark green head, chestnut breast, blackish shoulders and primaries, and pinkish-red bill. Males have a pronounced knob at the base of the bill in breeding plumage. Juveniles lack the dark green head and chestnut breast band, instead showing a dark-brownish head and rear neck, and a pale fore-neck.

Studies have shown that there is an excess of males in Shetland in spring. Females incubate their eggs in burrows, making them more vulnerable to predation by alien ground predators such as cats and feral polecat x ferrets. If the brood hatches, the female then has to contend with avian predators. Their success may depend on experience. One aggressive female was observed almost drowning a Great Skua that strayed too close to her ducklings, while another female looked on helplessly as a Great Black-backed Gull consumed all eight of her ducklings in just 45 minutes!

WHERE TO SEE

Favours relatively nutrient-rich lochs with adjacent improved grassland, and saltmarshes. The Loch of Spiggie, Loch of Benston and Loch of Collaster, Sandness, are important wintering sites but smaller flocks can be found throughout.

Wigeon

Rare breeding resident, common migrant and winter visitor.

The male is distinctive with its chestnut head, creamy forehead 'blaze', pink neck, grey body and black rear end. The rufous-toned female is best identified by her shape: a relatively large rounded head, small blue-grey bill, short neck and pointed tail. In flight the pointed wings, pointed tail and white belly are good features. More likely to be seen feeding on grass than other ducks.

The Wigeon's whistling 'wheeooo' call is much easier on the ear than the simple quacks made by most dabbling ducks, and a noisy flock can be heard at some distance. As with all ducks, the males take no part in rearing the ducklings. Once their partner has laid her eggs the males exchange their showy breeding plumage for an altogether more cryptic 'eclipse' plumage, allowing them to blend into their surroundings while they moult their wings – a period during which they become much more vulnerable to predators.

Gadwall

Scarce migrant in spring and autumn, with most in April and May. Occasionally winters.

Smaller and slimmer than Mallard. The male is grey bodied with a browner head and a black rear end. The female resembles a Mallard but shows clear-cut orange sides to its bill and its plumage is slightly colder. The belly is a cleaner white than in Mallard (apparent in flight and when up-ending) and in both sexes the white speculum (patch on the rear of the inner wing) is distinctive in flight.

Although a regular breeder in Orkney, Shetland still awaits its first breeding pair of this elegant dabbling duck. Dabblers prefer to feed with their eyes above the water, so that they can remain vigilant for predators. As food gets scarce, they are forced to take risks by up-ending, meaning their eyes are underwater. The Gadwall is more inclined than other dabblers to steal food from diving ducks. Female dabbling ducks lay large clutches of eggs, which can represent up to 70% of their body weight, and prior to egg-laying they eat more invertebrate food than males -- presumably they need more protein to manufacture the eggs.

WHERE TO SEE

*Found in small numbers
at many lochs,
in flooded fields and
wet boggy areas.*

Teal

Common breeding resident, migrant and winter visitor.

Small, with fast and agile flight. The male is distinctive with its chestnut head and green eye patches, greyish body and yellow under-tail. The female is essentially brown and mottled. Its small size, small bill (often with some orange at the base) and face pattern, with a darker eye-stripe and pale supercilium, enable identification.

The Teal is our smallest duck, weighing around 300 grams, and has a much lower life expectancy than other ducks, many living for just a year or two. Like many freshwater ducks, invertebrates form a large proportion of their summer diet, with seeds and plant matter more important in winter. Like all wildfowl, the female commences her three-week incubation when the last egg is laid ensuring that all the ducklings hatch at a similar time. They are quickly led away from the nest by the mother. Although they feed themselves she continues to brood them for a few days.

The rare **Green-winged Teal** (inset) from North America differs in having a vertical white stripe on the fore-flanks and a less well-marked pale line around the green face patch.

WHERE TO SEE
Anywhere with
fresh water,
and also occasionally
on the sea.

Mallard *(Stock Deuk)*

Common breeding resident, migrant and winter visitor.

Breeding males are distinctive, with a green head, narrow white collar, brown breast, grey body and black rear end. Eclipse males, females and juveniles are altogether more confusing. Typically, they show a strong face pattern, comprising a dark crown, pale supercilium and dark eye-stripe. The bill is usually greenish-yellow or orange. The body is boldly mottled brownish and the tail edged white. In flight appears heavy, with broad, relatively blunt-ended wings.

This very adaptable duck is much more tolerant of human presence than most wildfowl and is the ancestor of at least 20 of our varieties of domestic duck. Surprisingly, only the females quack! Its success is due in part to the female's willingness to nest some distance from water. This, however, can result in a marathon trek for her tiny ducklings when, immediately after hatching, she leads them to the safety of water. The egg yolk that they have retained doubtless helps them on this inaugural journey. Clutches can number up to 17 eggs, although these may involve two females laying in the same nest.

WHERE TO SEE
The nutrient-rich lochs
at Scatness, Hillwell
and Spiggie are
favoured haunts.

Pintail

Scarce migrant, occasionally appearing in winter. Has bred.

Like a slim, long-necked Mallard. The male is unmistakeable with its long, pointed central tail feathers, greyish plumage and chocolate-brown head and neck, with the white breast extending up the neck in a narrow stripe. The female shows a plain face and grey bill, scalloped greyish-brown body, slim neck and pointed tail. In flight, the white trailing edge to the inner wing stands out (female Mallard has two white bands in the wing), while the long wings, and longish neck and tail, contribute to a skinny, under-fed look.

The Pintail's long neck enables it to dabble (up-end) beyond the reach of other dabbling ducks. This species is prone to lead poisoning; lead shot from wildfowlers is ingested as it feeds among wetlands. Dabbling ducks ingest grit to help digest seeds and plant matter, and mistake the pellets for grit. Although lead shot has been banned in many European countries, it is still used in the UK. Pintails are also more susceptible to disease than other wildfowl and often feature prominently in major mortality events.

The south mainland lochs are the most reliable sites, especially Hillwell.

A Mallard-sized, dumpy, short-necked dabbling duck. The spatula-shaped bill is distinctive in both sexes. Males show bottle-green heads with a blackish back, white underparts and a bright chestnut patch on the flanks, and reveal a powder-blue forewing in flight. Females are scaly brown, with a less striking face pattern than Mallard.

*The **Garganey** (inset) is a rare visitor to Shetland. The male is distinctive with a striking white eye patch, contrasting with the brownish head, neck and breast, and pale greyish flanks.*

Shoveler

Scarce migrant and winter visitor, very rare breeder.

The Shoveler has a unique bill: it is spatula-shaped, longer than its head, and the tip is twice as wide as the base. Though it can 'shovel' directly into the mud, the Shoveler usually swings its bill from side to side as it feeds, straining food from the water using well-developed lamellae (small comb-like structures) along its edge. Its relatively straight flight makes it easier to shoot than many ducks, but it is apparently not favoured by wildfowlers due to the poor taste of its flesh.

WHERE TO SEE
The relatively nutrient-rich lochs
of the south Mainland,
Tingwall Valley and Nesting
offer the best chance.

Pochard

Formerly more common, now a scarce migrant and winter visitor.

A medium-large diving duck, slightly bigger than Tufted Duck. The chestnut head and neck, pale blue band on the bill, and grey body with a black breast and rear end, render males distinctive. Females and juveniles are duller with diffuse head markings, comprising a pale area above the base of the bill, and a pale eye-ring and line behind the eye, and greyish-brown bodies, with darker breasts and rear ends. The long, sloping forehead continues into the concave bill, giving a distinctive head-shape. They show a greyish wing-bar in flight.

Up to 250 Pochard spent the winter in Shetland in the mid-1970s but now it is scarce, occurring as individuals or in single-figure flocks. This decrease has been noted elsewhere in the UK but it is unclear whether it represents a real decrease in the population, or is a result of climate change. As the climate has become warmer in north-east Europe, birds do not need to move as far west as the British Isles in order to find suitable wintering conditions, choosing instead to remain further east, closer to their breeding grounds.

WHERE TO SEE

Found on a wider variety of freshwater lochs than other duck species but absent from nutrient-poor lochs on moorlands.

Tufted Duck

Common migrant and winter visitor.
The breeding population is increasing.

The male is distinctive with its crest, black head and body, and contrasting white flanks. The female shares the crest but is otherwise a uniform brown, with slightly paler flanks. Females and juveniles can show white around the base of the bill, and juveniles also lack the crest, which can lead to confusion with Scaup. Both sexes show a prominent white wing-bar in flight.

In the mid-1970s, around 1,000 individuals regularly wintered in Shetland, but less than half of that number is found here now. The breeding population, however, has increased markedly – a good example of how different populations of a species can show different trends. Like all ducks, females line their nests with their down which has good insulating properties. Males and females maintain a monogamous pair bond for the season, like most wildfowl. Less typical, however, is the tendency for some winter flocks to comprise predominantly males and others predominantly females. This may be related to different migration patterns or, more likely, different feeding strategies.

WHERE TO SEE

Often found among large flocks of Tufted Ducks.

Scaup

Scarce migrant and winter visitor.

Bigger than Tufted Duck with a larger, more rounded head, lacking a crest. The male also differs in having a grey mantle and back. Females and immatures can be tricky to tell from Tufted – concentrate on the bill and face pattern. Scaup show less black at the tip of the bill and lack a pale band behind this dark tip. They also show more white on the face (at the base of the bill) and often have paler cheek patches. Any sign of fine grey barring on the mantle, like the moulting male (above), confirm as Scaup. Both sexes show a distinct white wing-bar in flight.

The colour of bird feathers is produced by pigments and/or structural features that reflect light. It is these structural features that can make the head of a male Scaup look matt black, glossy green, or occasionally even glossy blue or purple. Scaup can often be seen rolling sideways in the water, a manoeuvre which enables them to preen and clean their feathers. Maintaining the condition of feathers is crucial for all birds, and the expression 'water off a duck's back' is testament to the waterproof qualities of well-maintained duck feathers!

**Found around most
of Shetland's coastline
often in large flocks
outside the breeding season.**

Eider *(Dunter)*

Common breeding resident.

A large diving duck. Adult males are distinctive with black caps, green napes and a combination of white breast and back, contrasting with black flanks and tails. Females are a cryptic, neatly-barred brown. Immature males are black, initially with a pale breast and circular spot at the rear flanks, but show more white as they get older. The short neck and heavy wedge-shaped head give Eiders a distinctive profile even at distance.

*The **Common Scoter** (inset) bred in Shetland until the mid-1990s, but is now a scarce migrant. It is usually seen on the sea, sometimes with Eiders. Males are black with yellow on the bill; females dark brown with pale cheeks and a dark cap.*

Shetland's Eider population has declined in recent years and their non-breeding distribution has changed, with flocks now forming at mussel rafts to take advantage of this new 'fast-food' source. Once mated the gaudy males congregate in large flocks offshore and moult into a drab eclipse plumage. The cryptic female rarely leaves the nest until the ducklings hatch, spending 99% of her time incubating the eggs, during which time she can lose up to 40% of her body weight! Females sometimes bring their ducklings together to form crèches in order to reduce the risk of predation. Each female leaves the crèche after a few days, presumably to get some much-needed food, and new females take over care of the crèche. Duckling mortality within a population is very high and as few as 10% may survive until the winter, but adults are long-lived for a duck. Some reach 30 years of age, although a life expectancy of ten is more typical. Eider down is well known for its insulating properties. Females cover their eggs with down when they leave the nest, but if scared off the nest they defecate on the eggs – the foul smell would put most potential predators off.

WHERE TO SEE

*Favours sheltered
sounds and voes.
Lerwick Harbour always
has a few in winter.*

Long-tailed Duck *(Calloo)*

Common winter visitor with a few usually remaining until June.

Adult males in winter plumage are distinctive with their long, pointed tails, black, grey and white plumage, dark neck patches, grey faces and pink on the bill. Immature males and females are more confusing but generally have brownish bodies with white flanks. The head and neck are whitish with, typically, a dark crown and face patch. In some plumages, however, the upperparts appear completely brownish, broken only by a white face patch.

Male Long-tailed Ducks are unique in that they have three distinct plumages each year. Their winter plumage is brightest and is equivalent to breeding plumage; breeding pairs form in the late winter when birds can be heard courting, with their beautiful 'calloo' calls. This is replaced with a more cryptic plumage before the breeding season and then an eclipse plumage after breeding has commenced. They are good divers and can reach depths of 60 metres, although most feeding is done at much shallower depths.

WHERE TO SEE

Occurs on freshwater lochs and in sheltered voes. The lochs of the south mainland and the south of Unst are regular winter haunts.

Goldeneye

Common winter visitor with occasional individuals remaining for the summer.

A medium-sized, dumpy duck with a relatively large, rounded head. The adult male is unmistakable, with its black and white body, and green head (looks dark at distance) with a large white spot on the lores. Females are greyish with a brownish head and limited white in the wing. The golden eye is obvious when close. Young males are similar to females but develop white on the body as they mature. In flight, the relatively uniform females and juveniles show two or three distinctive white patches on the inner wing.

Goldeneyes nest in holes and are well-known egg dumpers; some females lay their eggs in other females' nests. It is thought that this provides those females that are unable to secure a nest site with an opportunity to reproduce. The breeding population in Scotland increased markedly when nest boxes were supplied. The male's dramatic display, in which the head is drawn back to the middle of the back and then released vertically, often accompanied by a splash and a rasping double whistle, can be seen here on calm spring mornings.

J F M A M J J A S O N D

WHEN TO SEE

WHERE TO SEE

Sheltered voes such as Whiteness
and Weisdale are popular spots.
Also found on freshwater lochs
in the breeding season.

Red-breasted Merganser *(Herald Deuk)*

Scarce breeding resident and common winter visitor.

The Red-breasted Merganser and Goosander share a long, slim build and reddish bills which are much longer and thinner than our other common duck species. Drakes are relatively easy to identify: the Goosander is white bodied, often with a pink hue, with a dark-green head and blackish back; the Red-breasted Merganser shares the green head and black back, but has greyer flanks and a brownish breast.

The long, slender beak of this species has serrated inner edges which give this family the name sawbills. Like tiny backward-pointing teeth, these enable the birds to grasp their main prey item – fish. Small groups often swim along, repeatedly submerging their heads to look for food, and groups sometimes co-operate to force fish into shallower water where diving activity can become frenetic. They are one of the fastest-flying ducks, reportedly reaching speeds of 80mph.

J F M A M J J A S O N D

WHEN TO SEE

WHERE TO SEE

*Sheltered voes and
shallow freshwater lochs.
Weisdale Voe and Strand Loch
are good places to look.*

Goosander
Scarce migrant and winter visitor.

*Another sawbill but unlike the merganser the
Goosander is a hole nester. Although a common
breeding species in the northern half of the UK,
most arrive in Shetland when severe weather
occurs on mainland Europe, forcing birds west to
look for open water. On mainland Britain sawbills
come into conflict with fishing interests, as young
salmon and trout form part of their diet. They can
be shot under licence in the UK.*

Separating female and immature Goosander from
Red-breasted Merganser is more tricky. In
Goosander, the reddish head and neck is more solid
and has a more clear-cut lower border; the
upperparts and flanks are a cleaner grey than those
of the merganser, which show a brownish cast; the
crest is fuller, and the bill thicker at its base.

WHERE TO SEE

*Moorland with good
heather cover in the
central and west mainland.
Be prepared to walk a while.*

Red Grouse

Common but introduced, breeding resident.

The only grouse in Shetland. The size of a small duck, with a dumpy, round body and a small head. It has a fast, whirring flight action when disturbed, often accompanied by the 'go-bak, go-bak' call. Essentially brownish or rufous-brown plumage, the male showing red wattles over the eye.

It is unclear when grouse were introduced to the islands but Shetland birds are of the British race, so were brought from the mainland. The continental race – known as the Willow Grouse – moults into a white winter plumage, unlike those in Britain. The Red Grouse's diet is almost exclusively heather, although chicks take some insects as they require protein for growth. Like all grouse, the legs and feet are feathered. Grouse are shot less extensively in Shetland than in northern Britain, where managed Grouse Moors are the subject of much controversy. As well as being the emblem of the Famous Grouse whisky, the Red Grouse is also the logo of the monthly journal British Birds.

WHERE TO SEE

Sheltered coastlines and bays.
The bays at Quendale and South Nesting,
and the east side of Unst
attract good numbers.

Great Northern Diver (Immer Gös)

Common winter visitor, occasional individuals remaining in summer.

In winter plumage can only be confused with other diver species, Cormorants or Shags, but larger, with a stockier build, thicker neck and steeper forehead than any of these species. The upperparts appear dark, contrasting with a white chin, throat, fore-neck, breast and, if visible, flanks. The greyish dagger-like bill is held horizontally. Easier in summer plumage when bill black, blackish upperparts boldly chequered white, and black head and neck with a white-striped patch on the neck.

*Two or three **White-billed Divers** (inset) regularly winter in Shetland. Their yellowish-white bill, usually held above the horizontal, and paler brown head and neck differ from Great Northern.*

A leucistic (whitish) individual returned to winter in a west mainland voe annually from 1980 until 2000 illustrating that the species is faithful to wintering areas as well as breeding sites. This strong site fidelity means that local wintering populations can take many years to recover following a mass mortality event. During the Esso Bernicia oilspill in Shetland in 1979, 131 Great Northern Divers were found oiled in Yell Sound and Sullom Voe; the population there had only recovered to 20% of that level 35 years later. Divers have solid bones, unlike most birds, making them less buoyant when they hunt underwater for fish.

WHERE TO SEE

Breeds on small moorland pools and some larger lochs. Sheltered bays are best in winter.

Red-throated Diver *(Rain Gös, Loom)*

Common breeding summer visitor but scarce in winter.

Our smallest diver, looking a shade smaller than a Shag when settled on the water. In all plumages, the slim bill (invariably held pointing upwards at an angle), flat forehead and relatively slim neck should enable identification. Distinctive in summer plumage, with a grey head and neck, fine black-and-white-striped pattern on the hind neck, and brownish body. The maroon throat can often appear dark, leading them to be mistaken for Black-throated Diver – a rare bird in Shetland. The very white face and fore-neck, with a much narrower dark cap and hind-neck, help to distinguish from other divers in winter, although beware confusion with immature Shags and Cormorants. Divers do not leap clear of the water like these species often do.

Shetland is home to around 40% of Britain's breeding Red-throated Divers, and the species features prominently in local culture. The Old Norse name was Lómr and there are plenty of Loomi Shuns to be found on maps of Shetland. These are lochs where the divers did, and often still do, breed. It is also said that they foretold the coming of storms – "when the rain goose makes for the sea take up your boats and make for the lee, when the rain goose makes for the hill set down your boats and go where you will".

Red-throated Divers catch their fish at sea and can therefore breed on any loch, providing it is large enough for them to take off. They lay one or two eggs in a shallow scrape close to the water's edge. On larger lochs, waves generated by persistent strong winds can flood the nests, while changes in water levels can be a problem at small breeding lochs. An adult remains at the loch with the chicks when they are young, but older chicks may be left alone while both adults forage at sea.

WHERE TO SEE

*Common on coastal cliffs
and offshore but can
also be found inland,
notably in disused quarries.*

Fulmar *(Maalie)*

Abundant breeding resident.

Unmistakable when seen up close, with white underparts and pastel grey upperparts, dark eye shadow and a tube on top of the bill. Can be confused with gulls in flight but note the long, straight wings and stiff-winged flight, with shallow, rapid wingbeats followed by long periods of gliding, often just above the waves. In late autumn darker individuals known as blue Fulmars occur offshore.

The Fulmar is one of our longest-lived birds, some reaching 40 years of age. It takes seven or eight years for an individual to reach breeding age. The tube nostril, situated on top of the bill, enhances its sense of smell, and the pattern on this and the rest of the bill is unique to each individual. Don't get too close to their nests as both the adults and chicks spit foul-smelling oil as a defence mechanism. Fulmars didn't breed in Shetland until 1878, but following a massive population expansion they are now one of our most common seabirds, numbering

around a quarter of a million pairs. They feed by plucking items from the surface of the sea, and recent studies have found that many birds have a large volume of plastic pellets in their stomachs, sometimes leading to death. Fulmars spend much time gliding, which is very energy efficient, so they can cover large areas when searching for food. Competition for nest sites means they frequently come ashore during the winter months, and this often leads to arguments.

WHEN TO SEE

WHERE TO SEE

*Common offshore,
but rarely seen from land.
Join an organised night trip
to the colony on Mousa.*

Storm Petrel *(Alamootie)*

Common breeding summer visitor.

A tiny, House Martin-like seabird, rarely seen from land. Its blackish plumage is broken only by a square white rump patch and a white bar on the under-wing. The flight is fluttering, interspersed with occasional glides, and is always close to the surface of the sea.

This tiny seabird can live well into its twenties! It only visits its breeding colonies at night to avoid predatory skuas and gulls. As with most seabirds, the male and female share incubation and chick-rearing duties. Despite its small size, incubation takes around 50 days and the chicks take around ten weeks to fledge! Incubation shifts can last several days. Chicks are fed on a very rich stomach oil, which contains about twice the calories as the equivalent weight of a mars bar. They are capable of reducing their body temperature, and can even enter a state of torpor, if food is in short supply. By converting their planktonic prey into stomach oil, the adults can maximise the energy delivered in a feed.

With its yellowish bill, long neck and legs, dark crown and greyish body with whitish underparts the Grey Heron is unmistakable. In flight the neck is usually drawn in.

Shallow freshwater lochs and sheltered coastlines.

Grey Heron *(Hegri)*

Common autumn migrant but scarce at other times of the year. Has bred.

The Grey Heron has been the subject of the longest running survey by the British Trust for Ornithology (BTO); the first national census of heronries took place in 1928. Grey Herons are typically colonial and usually nest in trees; however, they have used cliffs on the rare occasions that they have bred in Shetland. Like all herons, their middle toe is pectinated (comb-like) and is used when scratching or cleaning the head, neck and bill.

WHERE TO SEE

A visit to the gannetries at Hermaness or Noss is an unforgettable experience but birds can often be seen from exposed coastal headlands or in sounds.

Gannet *(Solan)*

Abundant breeding resident.

Our largest seabird. Adults are distinctive with their yellow heads, white bodies and long, narrow wings of which the outer half are black. Juveniles are brownish, slightly paler on the underparts. They become whiter through successive moults, initially on the underparts and then on the back and wings, until they attain adult plumage in their fourth or fifth year. Even at a distance the shape and flight is distinctive, with shallow, uniform wingbeats interspersed with short glides.

Gannets have been more successful than most of Shetland's seabirds in recent years and their population continues to increase. They have a more varied diet and, with their large wingspan of up to six feet, are able to forage much further from their colonies. Young Gannets can be so well fed that they have to glide down to the sea and sit there for a few days until they lose enough weight to become airborne. Gannets are very aggressive and the geometric spacing of nests at colonies is no accident; each nest is situated just far enough from the next to reduce aggressive encounters. Feeding flocks can be spectacular, with birds diving arrow-like, with wings swept back, head first into the sea. To cushion the impact, they have air sacs in their face and chest, which act like bubble-wrap, while their nostrils are located within the mouth rather than on the outside.

J F M A M J J A S O N D

WHEN TO SEE

WHERE TO SEE

In shallow coastal waters, but heavily outnumbered by Shags. Large freshwater lochs, notably the Loch of Spiggie, harbour occasional individuals.

Cormorant *(Muckle Skarf, Loren)*

Scarce breeding resident.

Cormorants and Shags are easily confused though a significant size difference is evident when seen together. Cormorants are larger, with a thicker neck and bill, and a gently sloping forehead. The Shag has a thinner bill but a much steeper forehead. In breeding plumage Cormorants have extensive yellow facial skin, a white throat, white thigh patch and a purple-blue sheen. Some also show white on the sides of the neck. Adult Shags are crested, the yellow is restricted to the gape, they show a greener gloss and have no white in the plumage.

The Cormorant, like the Shag, is unusual among seabirds, as its chicks are born blind and naked. They also lay larger clutches than most seabird species. Incubation commences when the first egg is laid, so that the chicks hatch sequentially. When food is plentiful, four, or even five chicks may fledge, but in poor years the older, larger chick(s) commands most of the food. It has been argued that this strategy has evolved to ensure that at least one or two chicks fledge, even when the food supply is limited. In hot weather, fluttering of the large pouch of bare skin on the throat is a means of cooling down.

WHERE TO SEE

Nests on sea-cliffs
and common off exposed
and sheltered coastlines.
Rarely found on fresh water.

Shag *(Skarf)*

Common breeding resident.

Immature Shags have pale
throats and brownish bellies,
whereas immature Cormorants
tend to have the reverse pattern,
with dark necks and whitish
bellies. Cormorants often fly high
up, but Shags tend to stay close
to the sea. Shags, and to a lesser
extent Cormorants, leap clear of
the water when they dive.

*Shags build particularly large,
bulky nests in which they often
incorporate colourful or shiny
objects. One nest on Fair Isle
contained various screwdrivers
and spanners, presumably the
remnants of a tool set disposed
of by an islander. Adults appear
identical but the sexes can be
told apart by their calls – males
croak and females hiss. Flocks
of Shags and Cormorants are
often seen on rocks or
headlands with their wings
outstretched. There is still some
debate about whether this is to
dry out their wings or to aid
digestion. Shags use
their large, powerful feet for
underwater propulsion.*

WHERE TO SEE
*Shallow lochs with
emergent vegetation.
The Lochs of Spiggie and Hillwell
are favoured sites.*

Little Grebe

Scarce migrant and winter visitor. Has bred.

Considerably smaller than Teal. The very rounded, dumpy body, often showing a fluffy rear end, gives it a distinctive shape, and its frequent diving also assists identification. In winter shows a dark cap and back, with a buff face, throat and breast, and a paler whitish rear. In summer, the face and neck become a deeper chestnut and a prominent yellow mark appears at the base of the bill.

The lobed feet of grebes and divers are situated well back on their body, helping them swim underwater in pursuit of fish. The lack of a tail gives this species its fluffy back end. When it leaves its nest it covers the eggs with leaves and algae and, when young, the chicks will sit on the adult's back, peeping out from under its wings. Adults do a great disappearing act when spooked, swimming to the nearest vegetation where they remain invisible, with only their bills above the surface.

WHERE TO SEE

Favours shallow, sheltered voes and firths, and occasional on freshwater lochs. Tresta and Whiteness Voe support good numbers in winter.

Slavonian Grebe
Scarce migrant and winter visitor.

Larger than Little Grebe and the long neck, flattish head and longish body produce a more typical grebe shape. In winter appears very black and white, with black crown, rear neck and back/mantle contrasting with white face, fore-neck and underparts. Juveniles often retain remnants of dusky face stripes in early winter. The breeding plumage is much brighter with reddish neck and flanks, black head and body and stunning golden-yellow ear tufts.

The Shetland wintering population has quadrupled since 1980, almost certainly as a result of an increase in the Icelandic breeding population. It is known as the Horned Grebe in North America, due to the presence of erectile yellow tufts behind the eyes in breeding plumage. The species regularly eats its own feathers to form a matted plug in its stomach; this probably functions as a filter, and/or safely holds bones in the stomach until they can be digested. Parents even feed feathers to their chicks.

WHERE TO SEE
*Hunts for small songbirds
anywhere, including gardens.
Often roosts in undisturbed plantations,
such as Kergord or Sullom.*

Sparrowhawk

Scarce migrant and rare winter visitor.

Usually seen in flight, when small size, relatively short, rounded wings and long tail give characteristic outline. Flight comprises a series of rapid wingbeats followed by a short glide. When perched, the long tail is also obvious and the pale iris can be striking. Males have grey upperparts, with fine barring on whitish or rufous-toned underparts. Females are browner, as are immatures, which show much coarser markings on their underparts.

Females are up to 25% larger than males and weigh up to twice as much. The sexes therefore often take different prey species, reducing competition. During courtship and incubation, the male presents the female with food, and any prey he brings for the chicks is fed to them by the female. Sparrowhawks underwent a marked decline in Britain during the 1950s and 1960s as a result of the use of organo-chlorine pesticides, but they have recovered since the offending substances were banned. There is no evidence that Sparrowhawks have significant impacts on songbird populations, although this myth still persists.

J F M A M J J A S O N D
WHEN TO SEE

WHERE TO SEE
Can be seen in any open area, although more often around agricultural land.

Kestrel

Scarce migrant. Has bred.

The Kestrel is a medium-sized falcon with chestnut inner wings contrasting with darker outer wings. The underparts are buff, spotted darker. Adult males have a blue-grey head, rump and tail, but these are browner in females and immatures. The relatively long, pointed wings and longish tail are similar to other falcons but the Kestrel is the only one that habitually hovers. Glides much less frequently than the Sparrowhawk.

Kestrels prefer to hover, using their acute eyesight to detect prey, but will also hunt from perches which, although less costly in energy terms, is less successful. Like many birds, Kestrels can detect ultraviolet light. This enables them to locate small mammals, such as voles, that scent-mark their tracks with urine that reflects the ultraviolet light. A pair of Kestrels did breed in Shetland in 1992 but the absence of voles and scarcity of large insects in the islands prevents this being a regular occurrence.

WHERE TO SEE

*Breeds in heather moorland
but can be seen
anywhere at other times
of the year.*

Merlin *(Smyril, Peerie Hawk)*

Scarce breeding resident, migrant and winter visitor.

Slightly smaller than the Kestrel, with broader wings, heavier chest and a relatively shorter tail. Low, dashing flight when hunting, and often seen chasing small songbirds. Adult males show blue-grey upperparts and orange-toned underparts with fine streaking. Females and immatures show brownish upperparts with heavily streaked off-white underparts. The face is poorly marked, showing just an indistinct moustachial stripe.

In Shetland, Wheatear, Skylark and Meadow Pipit are the main prey species for this small falcon. Studies undertaken in the islands revealed that most nests that failed, did so at the egg stage, with elevated levels of mercury and organo-chlorines perhaps leading to infertility or thinning of the egg shells; they also showed that 18% of males but just 6% of females breed at one year of age. Two or more birds often undertake aerial play. This may strengthen the pair bond or help juveniles hone their hunting technique. In terms of length, this is Britain's smallest bird of prey, and in the glory days of falconry, the Merlin was considered very much a ladies bird.

WHERE TO SEE

Favours undisturbed coastlines, but can be seen anywhere.

Peregrine *(Stock Hawk)*
Rare breeding resident and scarce migrant.

Surprisingly similar in outline to Merlin when seen fleetingly. The larger size, deeper chest, more powerful flight and stronger head pattern become evident with more prolonged views. Adults have slate grey upperparts, neatly barred whitish underparts and a prominent black cap and moustachial stripe. Young individuals appear browner on the upperparts and more heavily streaked on the underparts – but still show a prominent face pattern.

The Peregrine is famed for its speed, supposedly reaching 200mph when stooping on prey. During World War II Shetland was one of the counties covered by the Destruction of Peregrine Falcons Order, whereby authorised persons could destroy Peregrines or their eggs to protect carrier pigeons. Some 25 pairs bred in Shetland in the 1950s, but then, in parallel with the rest of Britain, the population crashed due to the use of organo-chlorine pesticides. Despite a recovery elsewhere it remains a rare breeder in Shetland, possibly due to our remote location, or perhaps because of the abundance of Fulmars along our coastline. Juvenile Peregrines saturated in Fulmar oil have been found in Shetland on several occasions.

WHERE TO SEE
*Breeds in mires (swamps)
but migrants occur in
wet places with cover.
Often visits gardens in winter.*

Water Rail

Very rare breeding resident, scarce migrant and winter visitor.

Unlikely to be confused with anything else. The slender, reddish bill, long legs, relatively long neck and thin body, and habit of walking around in dense cover in wet areas, often with the tail cocked, give it a very distinctive appearance. Adults show brownish upperparts with black feather centres, greyish underparts with heavily barred flanks, and a buffy under-tail. Juveniles are similar but lack the grey on the neck and breast. If flushed, flies off weakly with dangling legs.

Generally a shy and retiring bird, its pig-like squealing can betray its presence. The body is flattened laterally, allowing it to move more easily through reeds and dense vegetation. Insects and plant material form most of the Water Rail's diet but they can be an aggressive predator and will take small birds if the opportunity arises. The dark markings on the under-tail are unique to each individual. When captured they sometimes play dead in the hope that the predator will release its grip.

WHERE TO SEE
Migrants can occur anywhere,
but favour Iris beds,
tall vegetation and
sand dunes.

Corncrake

Once a common breeding summer resident, but now a rare migrant with occasional breeding records.

More often heard than seen. If flushed, weak-looking flight, chestnut inner wings and dangling legs enable identification. The short, pinkish bill, greyish face and underparts, whitish-barred chestnut flanks, brownish wings and boldy marked upperparts are distinctive, though Corncrakes are rarely seen in the open.

*The rare **Spotted Crake** (inset) occasionally breeds in Shetland. It differs in its short yellow bill and white spots on the body and its preference for wet swampy areas.*

Shetlanders once thought that Corncrakes hibernated, but we now know that, despite their weak-looking flight, they are long distance migrants. Although very common here in the 19th century they had decreased markedly by the 1960s and ceased breeding annually in the 1980s. Changing agricultural practices have been implicated – notably the switch to earlier and more mechanised cutting of grass crops. Once assumed to be monogamous, recent research has revealed that the male often leaves before the eggs are laid and attempts to attract another female.

J F M A M J J A S O N D

WHEN TO SEE

WHERE TO SEE

Fresh water with a good
cover of emergent vegetation.
Always present at the
Loch of Hillwell.

Moorhen

Scarce but increasing breeding resident and migrant.

Size of a small duck, with distinctive shape, plumage and habits. Adults show a prominent red shield on the forehead, a red bill with a yellow tip, and long greenish-yellow legs. The plumage is dark greyish with a white line along the body and white sides to the under-tail. Juveniles appear greyish-brown with an off-white chin and throat. Moorhens are usually seen walking in damp areas near fresh water, with their tail held high or swimming with a somewhat jerking head motion.

Both sexes share incubation and chick-rearing, and the young leave the nest soon after hatching. They share their parents' long-toed but unwebbed feet that enable them to walk on floating vegetation. Both sexes have a prominent frontal shield, that varies in appearance with changing testosterone levels: the shield area increases in males, while the red is intensified in females. This may be important in courtship and territorial defence, serving as a sign of an individual's ability to fight.

Coot

Rare breeding resident, migrant and winter visitor.

The plump, rounded body, sooty black plumage and prominent white frontal shield and bill are distinctive. Coots usually swim on the water, up-ending or diving briefly for food, but will walk around on vegetation close to freshwater lochs when their large lobed feet can be seen. The eye is a deep red. Juveniles do not show the frontal shield and have a contrastingly paler chin, throat and fore-neck.

| J | F | M | A | M | J | J | A | S | O | N | D |

WHEN TO SEE

WHERE TO SEE
Shallow relatively
nutrient-rich lochs.
The Loch of Hillwell
is the most reliable site.

The white frontal shield has given rise to the saying 'as bald as a Coot'. The chicks hatch asynchronously (one by one), unlike most large birds that frequent wet habitats. The first chicks to hatch are led to the water by the male, while the female continues to incubate the remaining eggs. Adults can be very aggressive towards chicks. It had been argued that this aggression was to minimise sibling rivalry or to ensure that larger chicks survived when food was short. Recent research has revealed, however, that females without nests occasionally lay their eggs in other females' nests. It is these 'alien' chicks that are treated aggressively and they may starve to death.

WHERE TO SEE

*Occupies a wide range
of habitats in summer,
but favours damp,
improved grassland in winter.*

Oystercatcher *(Shalder)*

Common breeding summer visitor, but scarce in winter.

Unmistakable large wader, with black and white plumage, pink legs and carrot-like, straight, orange bill.

Despite its name this species does not eat oysters! They feed on a variety of prey, including earthworms, insect larvae and shellfish, with some adults specialising in a particular prey type. Whilst seasonal monogamy is typical of many waders, Oystercatchers are unusual as they often pair for life. They are also exceptional among waders as they provide food for their chicks up to, and sometimes beyond, fledging. Often silent while incubating, the adults become irritatingly noisy once their chicks have hatched. The Oystercatcher currently holds the longevity record for a British wader, with one individual reaching 40 years!

WHEN TO SEE

WHERE TO SEE

Favours grazed or wet margins of croftland, and moorland for breeding. Flocks often occur on croftland or damp, rough grassland at other times of the year.

Lapwing *(Tieves Nacket)*

Common breeding summer visitor, migrant and winter visitor.

A distinctive large, black and white wader with a long, thin crest. The dark upperparts show a beautiful green and purple iridescence in some lights. The face is black and white, a black breast band contrasts with the white underparts and the under-tail coverts are chestnut. In flight, the dark wings are broad and rounded with white tips and the underwing coverts are white. Juveniles and individuals in winter plumage show pale tips to the mantle and wing feathers.

Lapwing eggs were an expensive delicacy in Victorian Europe, with over 3,000 being taken annually from some estates in East Anglia. Research has shown that the species can produce up to four replacement clutches, each laid between five and twelve days after the previous one. Whilst the acrobatic courtship displays show off their chestnut under-tail, the noise of the beating wings is more dramatic. It is tempting to surmise that females are attracted to males with the largest crests but studies to date have failed to find any correlation between crest length and male quality. The species appears to be in decline in Shetland but is still faring better here than in most of Britain.

WHERE TO SEE

Favours moorland and blanket bog in the breeding season. Large flocks congregate on short improved turf at other times of the year.

Golden Plover *(Plivver)*

Common breeding summer visitor, migrant and winter visitor.

A medium-sized wader with a fairly plain face and short bill, but relatively long neck and legs. The upperparts usually appear a distinctly golden-toned brown. The underparts are extensively black in the breeding season but become whitish in the winter. The bill and legs are dark. In flight the rump is brownish but there is a narrow, diffuse whitish wing-bar. Ruff sometimes accompany Golden Plover but can easily be identified by their slightly longer bills and ochre-yellow legs.

The piping whistle and the aerial song flight of the male are among the most evocative sounds of a Shetland summer. They breed on moorland, even where heavily eroded. Eggs are laid at intervals of one to three days and incubation commences when the last egg is laid. The chicks start calling three to five days before leaving the egg and this may help synchronise hatching. Singing declines after egg laying and, given that some females leave the lion's share of the incubation and chick rearing to the male, this is perhaps not surprising. Other pairs divide their duties more evenly. In some, the male accompanies the first chicks to hatch and the female looks after the rest. In others, the female will do more of the brooding while the male remains on the look-out for predators. Like several other wader species the adults often feed outside of their breeding territories during incubation.

The **Grey Plover** (inset) is a scarce migrant and winter visitor to Shetland, best identified by its slightly larger size, heavier bill and distinctly grey-toned plumage. In flight it shows diagnostic black armpits and a white rump and wing-bar.

WHERE TO SEE

Favours bare areas of gravel or sand, including hill tracks, when breeding. Mostly found on damp, improved fields and sandy or pebble beaches in winter.

Ringed Plover *(Saandiloo)*

Common breeding summer visitor, migrant and winter visitor.

The only small wader likely to be seen in Shetland with greyish-brown upperparts, white underparts, a black and white head pattern and a complete, or near complete, black band running across the breast. The head markings and breast band are black in the breeding adults but browner in winter plumage adults and juveniles. The similar, but very rare, Little Ringed Plover has a distinct yellow eye-ring in all plumages and dull pink, rather than orange legs.

Many waders have especially adapted bills to locate their prey but Ringed Plovers feed mainly by sight. Look carefully and you will see them stand, watch, run forward and peck. Sometimes they tremble their feet on the ground, presumably to stimulate activity in their prey, perhaps replicating rain drops or the incoming tide. They are also masters at feigning injury, holding their wings as if broken, suggesting to a predator that they are an easy meal then flying away once it has been drawn away from the nest.

J F M A M J J A S O N D

WHEN TO SEE

WHERE TO SEE

*Favours low, rocky coastlines
and shingle beaches but flocks occur
on short, damp grassland especially
following rough weather.*

Turnstone *(Stenpikker)*

Common migrant and winter visitor that can be found year round.

A medium-sized wader whose short, slightly wedge-shaped bill, short orange legs and rather pied appearance enable easy identification. In breeding plumage shows broad chestnut fringes to the scapulars and wing coverts, and a more striking black and white head pattern. At other times of the year shows a fairly uniform darkish head, a broad, blackish breast band, dark upperparts and white underparts, appearing very black and white in flight.

Although present year round in Shetland, the Turnstone has never bred in the islands, or indeed in Britain. As it breeds at the same latitudes in coastal Norway this is perhaps surprising. As the name suggests, they will turn over stones to search for food, but they also use their bills to dig and probe, and even as a hammer to crack open shells. Individuals may specialise in certain food types, although social status may influence this as dominant birds may not allow a subordinate access to the same food.

WHERE TO SEE

*Breeds on blanket bog
and heathland. Migrants favour short,
damp grassland and, in autumn,
recently cut silage fields.*

Whimbrel *(Peerie Whaap)*

Common breeding summer resident and migrant.

*Shetland holds 95% of Britain's breeding
Whimbrel but the population in the islands has
declined by over 40% since the mid-1980s. Studies
in Shetland during the 1980s found breeding
densities of 11 to 21 breeding pairs per 100
hectares – among the highest in the world. The
species breeds on heathland and moorland, where
it likes to nest in tussocks, affording it a good view.
Chicks may be moved to adjacent reseeded or
improved grassland, which can be richer in
invertebrate food. The male's bubbling song flight
usually ceases once the eggs are laid.*

The Whimbrel is significantly smaller and darker than
the Curlew, with a straighter bill that is decurved nearer
the tip. The head pattern is diagnostic, with a dark eye-
stripe, pale supercilum, dark lateral crown stripes and a
pale crown stripe. Curlew can show a dark eye-stripe
and pale supercilium but are generally plainer faced.
In flight the Whimbrel is smaller with more uniform
darker wings, but the call is the best feature: a loud,
rapid whistling 'tu-tu-tu-tu-tu-tu'.

J F M A M J J A S O N D

WHEN TO SEE

WHERE TO SEE

Breeds on wet croftland, rough grassland, moorland edge and blanket bog. Outside the breeding season flocks occur almost anywhere.

Curlew *(Whaap, Spui)*

Common breeding resident, migrant and winter visitor.

Significantly larger and longer billed than Whimbrel with which it shares streaked, brownish upperparts, heavily streaked pale underparts and a large triangular white rump patch that extends up the back. The call, a classic mournful 'cur-loo', is very different to Whimbrel, and the song, although starting with a similar bubbling quality, does not end in a long drawn-out trill like that species.

The Curlew is Europe's largest wader. Unlike many waders, both the males and females perform the bubbling song flight and defend their territories. The long bill is curved downwards to maximise its chances of locating prey when probing intertidal mud. Prey species are usually oriented vertically, so a straight bill would have little chance of locating them. A curved bill allows a horizontal approach when inserting the bill vertically. If any vibration (from prey) is detected, rotation of the beak around its axis causes the tip to move in an arc through the mud, covering a wider area than would a straight bill.

WHERE TO SEE
Migrant flocks occur on short,
damp grassland and intertidal mudflats.
The Pool of Virkie can be
a reliable site in autumn.

Black-tailed Godwit
Rare breeding summer visitor and scarce migrant.

Contemporary accounts suggest that Black-
tailed Godwits were amongst the finest waders
for eating in Victorian times and hunting and
egg collecting, along with habitat change, saw
their demise as a British breeding species.
They have since recolonised but those
breeding in Shetland belong to the brighter
Icelandic subspecies. As is typical of waders,
chicks forage for themselves once they hatch,
hence their need to be born with well-
developed legs, feet and bill.

The two godwits are
much easier to separate
in flight: Black-tailed has
a white rump, black tail
and, most obviously, a
white wing-bar, whereas
Bar-tailed has plain wings
with a white rump and
finely barred tail.

WHERE TO SEE

Intertidal mud and sand,
and short, damp grassland.
The Pool of Virkie and Hamnavoe,
Yell, are reliable sites.

Bar-tailed Godwit

Scarce migrant and rare winter visitor, occasionally summers.

The two godwit species can be tricky to separate. Concentrate on structure; Bar-tailed has a distinctly shorter tibia (from knee to thigh), and a more noticeably upturned bill. In summer plumage Bar-tailed shows a more brick-red colouration extending to all of the underparts; Black-tailed has an orange neck and breast, and shows a more two-toned bill. Juvenile Black-tailed show a richer orange-buff neck and breast, and more patterned upperparts than Bar-tailed, but in winter plumage it is Bar-tailed that shows more strongly patterned upperparts, Black-tailed having more uniform grey upperparts.

Those that summer in Shetland are usually in their dun-grey winter plumage rather than their gaudy red summer plumage. These may be non-breeding birds which have no need to moult, or poor-quality individuals that cannot afford the energy required to moult. In either case it makes sense to remain in Shetland, rather than taking the added risk of migrating to the breeding grounds. This species now holds the avian record for long-distance non-stop flight, with one individual flying over 7,000 miles non-stop from western Alaska to New Zealand.

WHERE TO SEE

*Favours intertidal mud flats but also occurs
on damp turf on coastal headlands,
rocky coasts and damp grassland.
The Pool of Virkie is the most reliable site.*

Knot

Common migrant and scarce winter visitor.

Larger than Dunlin, with a stocky build, short, straight bill and relatively short legs. The bill is about the same length as the head. Winter plumage individuals and juveniles are best identified by their shape, grey-and-white plumage, pale supercilium and greenish-grey legs. In summer, the underparts become a rich orangey-red, which in combination with the structure, means the species is unlikely to be confused with anything else.

The Knot is a true long-distance migrant, with some individuals travelling over 9,000 miles from their high Arctic breeding areas to winter in New Zealand and South America. This requires the build-up of large fat reserves; birds can increase their body weight by up to 80% before they migrate. Like many tundra-breeding species, the reddish summer plumage is swapped for an altogether more austere dun-grey in winter. The colourful summer plumage breaks up the outline of the bird in its tundra breeding habitat, while the dull winter plumage blends in well with mud-flats.

J F M A M J J A S O N D

WHEN TO SEE

WHERE TO SEE

In autumn favours short, damp grassland, especially recently cut silage fields, but prefers wet areas with long vegetation in spring.

Variable in size, with largest males as big as Redshank and smaller females almost as small as Dunlin, although with longer neck and legs than that species. The bill is slightly longer than the head and slightly decurved, and legs vary from dull ochre-yellow to a more intense orange-yellow. Breeding males show much chestnut or black on head and breast, often forming a 'ruff'. Other plumages comprise spangled, brownish-black upperparts, plain underparts, often with a buff wash on the face, neck and breast, and a slight pale supercilium and darker cap.

Ruff

Scarce autumn migrant, but rare in spring. Has bred.

Males are much larger than females and possess a colourful, but variable, breeding plumage. The Ruff is unique among British waders in having a lek-based mating system. Males are promiscuous, gathering at traditional lekking (display) arenas and mating with as many females as they can. Females may nest near the lek site, or move considerable distances before nesting. The female takes full responsibility for building the nest and raising the young.

Curlew Sandpiper

Scarce migrant, mainly in autumn.

Most easily confused with Dunlin, but slightly larger with longer legs and a longer, more decurved bill. The vast majority of Shetland records refer to juveniles. They show a peachy wash on the breast and generally appear much cleaner on the underparts than juvenile Dunlins, which show significant streaking. Adults have brick red underparts in summer, and in winter the species becomes dun-grey on the upperparts and white on the underparts. The white rump and wing-bar are useful separating features in flight. The bill and legs are black.

The lemming (a small furry rodent) is a key species in the ecology of parts of the high Arctic. When lemmings are abundant they form the chief prey of the Arctic Fox during the short summer. In years when lemming are less numerous, however, Arctic Foxes prey heavily on waders and ducks, causing reduced breeding success in those species. The number of Curlew Sandpipers (and some other waders) arriving in Shetland in a particular autumn can, therefore, depend heavily on the population of lemmings in the Arctic in the preceding summer.

Sanderling

Common migrant. Found every month of the year, but rare in winter.

A smallish wader, similar in size to Dunlin, but shows a shorter, straighter black bill and often a more active feeding behaviour, consisting of rapid runs. Larger than Little Stint, with which it shares its short, straight black bill. In summer plumage shows reddish tones to face, throat and neck. The Juvenile has neatly-spangled, black-and-white upperparts, and white underparts. In winter appears a uniform pale grey on upperparts with white underparts. In flight, shows a much stronger white wing-bar than Dunlin.

Running along a sandy beach in advance of breaking waves, Sanderlings resemble tiny clockwork toys. Each wave brings a new source of food. The breeding season in the high Arctic can be short and some females do not lay eggs until late June or early July. Like the Knot, the autumn migration through Shetland often shows two separate peaks. Some adults, including failed breeders, move through in late July, while some successful breeders and juveniles pass through four weeks later, in late August and early September.

WHERE TO SEE

Breeds on blanket bogs but otherwise favours intertidal mudflats, sandy beaches and coastal headlands washed with salt spray.

Dunlin *(Plivver's Page)*

Common breeding summer visitor, migrant and winter visitor.

The most common small wader in Shetland. Dumpy with relatively short legs and a slightly decurved bill of variable length. Summer plumage comprises warm brown upperparts and a diagnostic black belly patch. Juveniles have dark brown upperparts with neat rufous edgings to their feathers, and white underparts with dark streaks on the breast and fore-flanks, but moult into a dun-grey winter plumage. The bill and legs are black.

This loosely-colonial species is a better indicator of high-quality blanket bog (peatland) than any other in Shetland. Pairs often return to the same breeding site each year. The male performs a high aerial song flight, which often stimulates other nearby males to sing. The Shetland name is derived from their habit of appearing close to an alarming Golden Plover. Like most waders, incubation commences once the last egg of the clutch is laid. This ensures that the chicks hatch at roughly the same time. As with all waders the chicks are precocial, meaning their eyes are open and they are covered in down when they hatch. The chicks can feed themselves soon after hatching but need regular brooding for a few days until they can maintain their own body temperature.

J F M A M J J A S O N D

WHEN TO SEE

WHERE TO SEE

*Rarely seen away
from low rocky coasts
and associated
sandy beaches.*

Purple Sandpiper
Common migrant and winter visitor.

Slightly larger and dumpier than Dunlin but with a similar bill shape. The orange base to the bill and orange legs, combined with its preference for rocky coastlines, should enable identification. The upperparts are dark with some paler fringing, and the underparts are off white with dense streaking across the breast, becoming less heavy on the flanks. The head pattern is quite subdued with some individuals showing an indistinct supercilium and others just a pale spot in front of the eye.

Shetland hosts some 7% of the British wintering population of Purple Sandpipers. Small flocks run swiftly over rocks, turning over debris and searching crevices for food items. Some individuals will even submerge under small waves briefly to snap up food. The species is less migratory than other northern waders, remaining as far north as possible in winter. On the breeding grounds the female often departs just before the eggs hatch, leaving the male to care for the young.

J F M A M J J A S O N D

WHEN TO SEE

WHERE TO SEE

The Pool of Virkie is the most reliable site but can be found on beaches, salt spray-washed headlands and wet pools.

Little Stint

Scarce migrant, mainly in autumn.

Tiny, about two-thirds the size of Dunlin, with short, straight, black bill. Juveniles show obvious white 'tram-lines' down their mantle, and their upperpart feathers and tertials show blackish centres with bright rufous fringes. The underparts are white with some fine streaking and warm colouration evident on the sides of the breast. Adults in summer plumage (right) show rusty tones on the head, breast and upperparts, but in winter they become grey and white. Take care not to confuse with Sanderling.

Although the high Arctic breeding season lasts just a few weeks, there is often a short-term super abundance of food, as midges, craneflies and other insects hatch en masse. The Little Stint will often lay two clutches of eggs to take advantage of this abundant food source. The male incubates the first clutch while the female lays the second. She then takes over the first leaving him to incubate the second.

Red-necked Phalarope *(Peerie Deuk)*

Scarce breeding summer visitor and rare migrant.

Slightly smaller than Dunlin, with very fine, short, needle-like bill. Adult females show a white throat and white spot above the eye, with a dark greyish face and extensive red on the neck sides. The crown, rear neck and breast is grey and the mantle and back are dark with golden 'tram-lines'. Males (above) are similar but duller, often showing much reduced red on the neck and throat. Juveniles (opposite) have a dark crown and dark eye-patch, dark upperparts with prominent golden stripes, and whitish underparts. Although often seen swimming, phalaropes will also search for food on foot.

Shetland is THE place to observe this wader in the UK, although huge populations breed further north. The RSPB has been working hard in Shetland to create suitable breeding habitat for phalaropes, which comprises a mosaic of fresh water and emergent vegetation. Phalaropes are one of the few waders that habitually swim. In summer, insects form an important part of their diet and the larvae of many of these are aquatic. The emerging adults often climb out on to stones that protrude above the water to dry their wings. The phalaropes can be seen picking these insects from such stones.

Recent research has shown that Shetland's breeding phalaropes, winter in the Galapagos Islands! Sexual role reversal is complete in this species; the more colourful female will form a brief pair bond with two or more males, and the males are left to incubate the eggs and rear the chicks.

Breeds on the rocky shores of larger lochs
or burns, mainly in the central
and north mainland. Migrants favour
coastal pools and low shorelines.

Common Sandpiper

Scarce summer breeding visitor and migrant.

A medium-sized wader, most easily identified by its distinctive behaviour and shape. It has a very horizontal body position, often appearing almost to crouch, and relatively short neck and legs, but a long tail. The upperparts are a brownish-grey and a distinct greyish breast band is separated from the wing by an area of white that extends into white underparts. The straight bill shows a paler base and is slightly longer than the head, which shows an indistinct supercilium. The legs are a dull greenish-grey. Its flight is very distinctive comprising rapid, stiff-winged, shallow, almost flicking wingbeats interspersed with short glides.

The almost constant bobbing up and down of the head and body, and pumping of the tail, make this bird very distinctive. This behaviour is reflected in its local name Matakakoni in Papua and New Guinea which translates as 'the wader that walks a little, then copulates'. As with many duck and wader species it has a close counterpart on the other side of the Atlantic: the Spotted Sandpiper is, as its name suggests, heavily marked with dark spots in summer, but separating the two in non-breeding plumage is altogether more challenging.

| J | F | M | A | M | J | J | A | S | O | N | D |

WHEN TO SEE

WHERE TO SEE
Pools, wet ditches and burns.
The burn at Quendale mill
is a good bet in
early autumn.

Green Sandpiper

Scarce migrant, mainly in autumn.

A relatively long-legged and long-necked wader but smaller than a Redshank. The upperparts are dark blackish with a contrasting white rump, and the underparts whitish with dense streaking on the breast forming a clear breast band. The dark bill is longish, about 1.5 times the head length, and the pale supercilium does not extend back behind the eye. The legs are greenish. Distinctive black-and-white appearance in towering escape flight, during which it utters classic 'twit-a-wit' call repeatedly.

*The **Wood Sandpiper** (inset) is a scarce migrant, mainly in spring. It differs in its yellow legs, browner upperparts, prominent supercilium, extending behind the eye, and paler underwing.*

More solitary than most waders, Green Sandpipers prefer freshwater habitats year round. Their distinctive escape flight when flushed comprises a rapid zig-zag and towering climb. Their nesting habits are even more exceptional, as they lay their eggs in trees, usually in the old nest of a crow, pigeon or thrush, or even a squirrel's drey. Migration often occurs at night and occasionally one can be heard calling as it flies over on an early autumn evening

WHERE TO SEE

*Breeds on blanket bog.
Migrants favour loch edges,
wet pools and
intertidal areas.*

Greenshank

Rare breeding summer visitor and scarce migrant.

Larger than Redshank, with longer, slightly upturned bill. The bill base and legs are greenish. In summer plumage has brownish-grey upperparts with some darker feather centres, and white underparts with extensive streaking on the head, neck and breast. Juveniles and winter adults show greyer upperparts with neat pale fringing, white underparts with finer streaking on the head, neck and upper breast, and a more pronounced pale supercilium. The white triangle on the back and uniform brown wings are obvious in flight. Call a distinctive triple whistle 'chew-chew-chew'.

The population of Greenshank in the Flow Country of Sutherland was subject to one of the most celebrated ornithological studies. Eight members of the Nethersole-Thompson family studied the species there for half a century. For six weeks every summer from 1964 to 1978, the family (and guests) lived in their Greenshank Camp – a wooden fishing hut measuring about five metres by three metres. Two separate monographs, published in 1951 and 1979, detailed much of their work.

WHERE TO SEE

Wet areas, with tall vegetation are typical breeding haunts. At other times can be found almost anywhere where it is wet, inland and along the coast.

Redshank (Kjoorlie)

Common breeding resident, migrant and winter visitor.

A medium sized, long-legged wader with a medium-length bill. Its bright red legs are shared only with the Spotted Redshank – a rare visitor to the islands. In flight has distinctive, broad, white trailing edge to the inner wing and a wedge-shaped white rump. Calls frequently when flushed, a loud whistling 'teeu-who-who'. The summer plumage (below) is more heavily marked than the plainer winter plumage (above).

One of our most nervous and wary waders, yet when the chicks hatch, it quickly becomes one of our noisiest! Some adults weave a canopy over their nest, presumably as a form of camouflage. Redshanks often breed in close proximity to one another and regularly nest near Lapwings, taking advantage of that species' aggressive nature towards predators. They often pair for life. Females sometimes leave the chick-rearing duties to the male, while they lay a second clutch. The breeding population in Shetland is in decline.

The **Spotted Redshank** (inset) has a slightly longer bill, with a hint of a droop at the tip, and prominent white lores when in juvenile or winter plumage. Breeding adults are predominantly black.

WHERE TO SEE
*Vegetated wet areas, muddy patches, burns and ditches.
Often occurs with Snipe, but in much smaller numbers.*

Jack Snipe

Common autumn migrant, scarce in winter and spring.

Only two-thirds the size of a Snipe and flushes silently, often only when almost trodden on, with more level flight. The bill is also shorter than Snipe – about 1.5 times the length of the head – compared to twice the length in Snipe. When seen close shows darker upperparts than Snipe, with brighter golden tram-lines.

When feeding, Jack Snipe often rhythmically bob their body up and down, as if it was set on springs. Observing this behaviour, however, is a real challenge. Their cryptic plumage makes them very hard to see on the ground and they will often allow an approach to within just a few feet before flying off. Like many other waders, the bill tip is very soft and pliable, making it very sensitive when searching for prey.

Woodcock
Common migrant and scarce winter visitor.

Woodcock are rarely seen in the open. The plumage is cryptic: essentially a barred brownish, with distinct dark marks over the head. Usually flushes noisily from close quarters, when large, rotund appearance, with broad wings, is distinctive, appearing like an over-sized Snipe. The rufous rump is obvious as it flies away. Flight much heavier and less jinking than that of Snipe.

WHERE TO SEE
Under-recorded
as favours heather moorland
but can be found almost anywhere
with sufficient cover.

In the early 1930s this species was shot extensively on Fair Isle to supplement the islanders' income. Over a dozen men took part, with the best shots bagging in excess of 200 birds each year. They were shipped south to Edinburgh and Glasgow and apparently fetched around one and a half shillings each. The London markets proved more lucrative, however, paying an average of three shillings each, and up to four and a half shillings for the best quality birds. A few are still shot in the islands for personal consumption.

WHERE TO SEE

*Breeds on wet croftland,
moorland margins and blanket bog.
Found in damp habitats when
migrating or in winter.*

Snipe *(Horsegok, Snippik)*

Common breeding summer visitor, migrant and winter visitor.

Its cryptic plumage, harsh calls when flushed, and zig-zagging escape flight mean that the Snipe is unmistakable. Differences from Jack Snipe are given under that species. On the rare occasions it is seen on the ground, the long, straight bill, dumpy shape, typically crouching posture and boldly-striped brown-black-and-buff plumage are distinctive.

It is the complex and intricate pattern of blacks, browns and buffs that enables the Snipe to remain camouflaged and often invisible to the human eye. Once flushed, its rapid and erratic flight provides one of the greatest challenges for wildfowlers. Males typically arrive back on territory one or two weeks before the females and commence their characteristic drumming display, which is such a feature of a warm spring or summer evening in Shetland. The drumming noise is actually produced by air passing through the outer tail feathers during steep dives. Both sexes can be promiscuous until

the pair bond forms and eggs are laid, and males will continue to seek out unattended females until the chicks hatch. The male often cares for the first chicks to hatch, leaving the female to wait and care for the remainder of the brood, and the pair may not make contact again. The territory may then be taken over by another male. The Snipe's eyes are situated on the side of its head enabling it to see through 360°, giving it an early warning if predators approach.

WHERE TO SEE

Blanket bog and heathland is the favoured breeding habitat. Probably best looked for at the larger seabird colonies on Fair Isle, Foula, Hermaness, Mousa and Noss.

Arctic Skua *(Skootie Aalin)*

Common, but rapidly declining, breeding summer visitor.

Much smaller and slimmer than Great Skua. Like a dark gull, but with white primary patches, very pointed wings and projecting central tail feathers. Two colour morphs: dark individuals are all dark, sometimes with a slightly paler face; pale individuals show a dark cap, upperparts and wings, contrasting with white face, collar and underparts, with a broken dusky breast band and dusky under-tail. Juveniles are a mottled, warm brownish with white wing patches and pointed central tail feathers that barely project beyond the tail.

The Arctic Skua is a kleptoparasite: it chases other birds, forcing them to drop or disgorge their food, which it then steals. Kittiwakes, Arctic Terns and Puffins are its main targets, all of which are experiencing problems obtaining enough food in Shetland waters, so it is not surprising that Arctic Skua populations, too, are in decline. Those few chicks that do fledge often succumb to Great Skuas during their first tentative flights. Adult Arctics, however,

are much more agile than Great Skuas and will dive upon and strike their larger cousins. They are also very aggressive towards human intruders and will often clip the back of an observer's head if they stray too close to the nest. Arctic Skuas come in two colour morphs: about 20% of Shetland breeders are pale morphs and 80% dark morphs. The proportion of pale morphs increases with latitude, although as yet there is no satisfactory explanation as to why this is the case.

The much rarer **Long-tailed Skua** (inset) occasionally passes through Shetland in late spring. Adults are distinctive because of their very long central tail feathers, but they are difficult to distinguish in other plumages.

Great Skua *(Bonxie)*

Common breeding summer visitor.

When perched, the Bonxie can be separated from similar-sized immature gulls by its all dark, mottled-brown plumage. In flight its white wing patches are distinctive. The smaller and slimmer Arctic Skua shares its white wing patches, but its plumage is more uniform and the adults have distinctly longer central tail feathers.

The Great Skua is Shetland's most important bird in a global context, with 40% of the world population breeding here. It provides something of a conservation conundrum, however, as in recent years it has switched prey from sandeels to other seabirds, and predation by Great Skuas has undoubtedly played a role in the demise of both Arctic Skua and Kittiwake populations in the islands. Individual Great Skuas will set up feeding territories within Puffin colonies and in recent years they have been observed killing adult Gannets! Cannibalism of chicks, too, has become a feature in years when food is scarce. There is some evidence to suggest that the Great Skua is a relative newcomer to the northern hemisphere; our seabirds may therefore be more vulnerable to its depredations as they have not co-evolved with it.

93

J F M A M J J A S O N D
WHEN TO SEE

WHERE TO SEE
Hermaness, Noss and Sumburgh Head
are good places to look but present
around much of Shetland's
more exposed coastline.

Puffin *(Tammie Norie)*

Common breeding summer visitor.

Adults in summer plumage are unmistakable. The face patch is grey in winter when the adult's bill is less colourful and the juvenile's bill is smaller and darker. The flight is fast and whirring like all the auks. The Puffin is distinctly smaller than the Guillemot and Razorbill in flight, with a darker underwing and no white trailing edge to the wing.

Many of the Puffins observed at colonies are non-breeders, between two and five years of age. They visit the colony to learn the social behaviours necessary to breed. Breeding adults can reach in excess of 20 years of age. Puffins are monogamous and, after a long winter spent apart at sea, reunite at the colony in spring. Courtship follows, often involving bill rubbing. The single white egg is laid in the darkness of a burrow, or under a rock.

It therefore has no need for a complex pattern, like those found on the eggs of our other auks, in order to aid recognition. Sandeels are the preferred food for chicks and an adult Puffin can easily carry ten or more in its specially-adapted bill. They have

surprisingly sharp claws, useful for excavating a burrow if none are available. The Puffin chick (above) leaves the burrow six to seven weeks after hatching when it is the same size as, and independent of, its parents.

WHERE TO SEE

Well distributed around more exposed coastline where they breed in loose aggregations. Feeding flocks often congregate in sounds and sheltered bays outside the breeding season.

Black Guillemot *(Tystie)*

Common breeding resident.

Unmistakable in summer when the oily-black plumage is broken only by a large white wing patch. In winter takes on a grey and white appearance, the adult having a pure white wing patch, and those in their first winter showing dark markings within their white wing patch. Tysties are smaller than Guillemots and Razorbills, being closer in size to a Puffin. The white wing patch is diagnostic in flight.

Watching and listening to a gathering of displaying individuals on the sea, flashing their white wing patches, is a memorable experience. Unlike our other auks, which all lay a single egg, the Tystie lays a clutch of two. This may be a product of it having a more reliable food source – it feeds on a wide variety of inshore fish found in shallower water. In bird species, clutch size has evolved to deliver the maximum number of chicks over the lifetime of an adult. Seabirds are generally long-lived with low reproductive outputs. In years when they are in poor body condition many seabirds will not attempt to breed – it makes no sense to risk the additional stress of breeding which could result in **death; it is better to ensure survival for future breeding seasons. The Tystie is the emblem of the Shetland Bird Club.**

Small numbers can be found at most large seabird colonies. Look in nooks and crannies in the rock face and among boulders.

Bill diagnostic, with laterally flattened appearance and single white horizontal and vertical lines. Slightly smaller than Guillemot, with blacker upperparts, clean white flanks and more pointed tail. Juveniles and young birds show a smaller and less blunt bill. Very difficult to identify in flight but appears dumpier and shows more white on the sides of the rump than Guillemot.

Razorbill
(Sea Craa, Wylkie)

Common breeding summer visitor but scarce outside breeding season.

Like most seabirds, Razorbills are monogamous. They share parental duties and raise their chick together. They may, however, be unfaithful as males visit leks (mating areas) near the colony where females seek extra-pair copulations. Each of our four breeding auk species has a different bill structure and occupies a slightly different niche. Razorbills can carry four or five fish across their bills. Like other auks, they feed by pursuing fish under water, flapping their powerful wings. The male accompanies the flightless chick away from the colony and it takes this opportunity to moult, losing all its wing feathers in quick succession so that it too becomes flightless. One BTO-ringed Razorbill lived to the ripe old age of 41 years!

WHERE TO SEE

Large numbers can pass headlands like Sumburgh Head but better views are likely to be obtained in sounds and sheltered bays.

Little Auk *(Rotchie)*

Scarce winter visitor.

Little Auks are tiny - only half the size of a Puffin - and can be very difficult to see on the water. Their winter plumage is essentially black and white, and their tiny bill is hardly noticeable. When sat on the water they appear to have an almost white collar. When feeding they will dive frequently, and often give the impression of dragging their wings on the sea. The whirring flight with rapid wingbeats is typical of auks but they tend to jink from side to side more than the larger auks. The white trailing edge is difficult to see in flight.

The number of Little Auks reaching Shetland waters in winter depends largely on the wind direction, with more occurring in northerly winds. Occasionally, in severe weather, Little Auks can be found inland, mistaking wet roads for water bodies, or even accompanying flocks of migrant Starlings! In some parts of the high Arctic where Little Auks breed they are considered a delicacy. The Greenland Inuit make kiviaq – a seal skin stuffed with 300-500 Little Auks, closed together with seal fat and left to ferment for 3-18 months under a pile of rocks!

Guillemot *(Longwi, Loom)*

Abundant breeding summer visitor but scarce outside the breeding season.

Nests in dense colonies where longish, pointed bill, brownish-black head, neck and underparts and white underparts, with dark 'barcode' along the flanks, enable easy identification. Around 25% of Shetland birds are 'bridled', showing a white line extending back from the eye. In winter plumage (above), the face and neck become white, with a darker mark running down behind the eye and a dusky half-collar. The browner-toned upperparts and the 'barcode' along the flanks also differ from Razorbill. The large size and lack of a white wing patch separates from Black Guillemot year round.

Superficially Guillemots look like penguins – a case of convergent evolution where unrelated species have evolved to look the same because they occupy similar niches. Guillemots nest in dense colonies on open ledges, where their calls and behaviour (social skills) are crucial in maintaining harmony. Guillemots hold fish lengthways in the bill when bringing them to their chicks. Chicks fledge at just three weeks of age, while still flightless and only a third the size of the adult. The male calls to the chick from the sea when it is time to fledge and the two swim out to the Norwegian coast together. It was believed that the Guillemot's egg shape had evolved so that if it is accidentally knocked, the egg will turn in a circle rather than roll off the ledge. A more plausible explanation is that this shape allows the maximum transfer of heat from the adult's body to its egg during incubation. Guillemots have been recorded at depths of 180 metres, although most feeding is in much shallower water than this!

WHEN TO SEE

WHERE TO SEE

*Anywhere coastal
but usually in sheltered bays.
Annual at the
Pool of Virkie.*

Sandwich Tern

Scarce summer visitor.

Larger than Arctic and Common Tern with a narrow, longish black bill with a yellow tip, and a different shape in flight, with longer, narrower wings and shorter tail. The upperparts are a pale grey and the underparts white, giving it a much whiter look than Arctic and Common Tern. The black cap ends in a shaggy crest. The outer four or five primaries are often darker than the inner-wing producing a dark wedge in flight. Legs black. The forehead becomes white in late summer as moult to winter plumage commences.

Despite breeding in small colonies in Orkney, the Sandwich Tern is a scarce visitor to Shetland. At breeding colonies it is positively timid compared to its smaller cousins, the Arctic and Common Tern. It often nests in close proximity to other tern species and gulls and perhaps benefits from their aggressive reaction to predators. The species is named after the small seaside town in Kent where it was discovered over 200 years ago.

Breeds on beaches, offshore skerries and holms, often among Arctic Terns.

Common Tern *(Tirrick)*

Scarce summer breeding visitor.

With their long tail streamers, buoyant flight, black caps, greyish upperparts and white underparts, terns are distinctive birds, but separating Common from Arctic Tern is always a challenge. When perched, Common shows a more orange-red bill usually with a distinctly blackish tip, although beware Arctic can show a dark tip too. Common also has slightly longer legs although this is rarely useful unless the two are stood together. Flight identification and the identification of juveniles are dealt with under Arctic Tern.

The Common Tern feeds by plunge diving into the surface layers of the sea and will often drink on the wing. They breed in a wider range of habitats than other terns and in mainland Britain have readily taken to artificial floating rafts on fresh water for nesting. Common Terns are monogamous, like most seabirds, and one study showed that nearly 80% of pairs remained together for at least two seasons. Common and Arctic Terns do not breed until their second summer, and less than 1% of one-year old birds return to the breeding colonies. Why risk the lengthy migration north to the breeding grounds, when you cannot breed?

WHERE TO SEE

*Breeds on bare areas inland
and on beaches, skerries
and offshore holms.
Colonies are often transient.*

In flight, Arctic Terns differ from Common Terns structurally and in plumage. They have relatively narrower, more pointed wings and longer tails, and appear to have less head and neck projecting beyond the wings than in Common Terns. This gives them a more petite, streamlined look. The upper-wing of Arctic Tern always appears a clean grey throughout its length, whereas Common Tern inevitably shows a dirty, dark wedge in its mid or outer primaries. The underwing also differs: Arctic Tern shows a neat, thin, black trailing edge to its primaries whereas Common Terns shows a thicker, less well-defined black trailing edge. These underwing differences are also evident in juvenile plumage, when Arctic also looks whiter on the underwing than Common. On the upper-wing, juvenile Arctic shows much whiter primaries and secondaries (rear-wing) than Common, which appears a darker grey, with a dark bar across the secondaries. A few weeks after fledging Arctic Terns show an all-dark bill, whereas Common Terns usually retain a reddish base to their bill.

Arctic Tern *(Tirrick)*

Common summer breeding visitor.

Arctic Terns see more sunlight than any other species as they breed at high latitudes and winter deep in the southern hemisphere. Some individuals fly 50,000 miles over the course of a year; the equivalent of flying to the moon and back over a lifetime! Arctic Terns are among the most aggressive parents, dive-bombing any potential predators, and it is not unusual for them to draw blood if you stray too close to their chicks. They have suffered from the recent shortages of sandeels in Shetland waters more than any other seabird, probably because they have a smaller foraging range than other species and can only feed in the surface layers of the sea. The arrival of this species, perhaps more than any other, defines the start of true spring in Shetland, with the first birds returning in early May.

WHERE TO SEE

Breeds on sea-cliffs; Noss and Sumburgh Head have small colonies. Usually seen in sounds and sheltered bays in winter. Rare inland.

Kittiwake *(Weeg, Rippack Maa)*

Common but rapidly declining breeding species, common migrant and winter visitor.

A smallish gull with pointed wings and buoyant, tern-like flight. Shares yellow bill, grey upperparts and white underparts with Common Gull, but black legs and solid black, 'dipped-in-ink' wing tips differentiate it from that species. Adults show a dark, dusky mark at the rear of the face, and a greyish nape in winter. Juvenile and first-winters show a black W-pattern on the wings, a black tail band and a black half-collar.

Nests are built on narrow ledges, making this Britain's only truly cliff-nesting gull. The name Kittiwake is onomatopoeic, relating to its call, while its scientific name tridactyla, *refers to the fact that it only has three toes. The Shetland population declined from 55,000 pairs in 1981 to just 5,000 in 2014! A shortage of their favoured prey – the sandeel – and an increase in predation by Great Skuas are largely responsible. Recent satellite tracking has revealed that some Shetland birds spend the winter on the other side of the Atlantic, off Newfoundland.*

WHERE TO SEE

Breeds inland in wet areas with long vegetation and on island holms. Colonies can change from year to year. More coastal in winter when often congregates at salmon farms, but also found inland.

Black-headed Gull *(Hoodie Maa)*

Common breeding summer visitor, migrant and winter visitor.

In summer, the dark chocolate-brown hood is distinctive. In winter, the bill loses its deep-red tone, becoming more orange-red, and the hood is replaced by two dark spots on the side of the face. Juveniles have extensive brown markings on the back and wings, with the back becoming grey in first-winter plumage. The combination of a white leading edge to the outer wing and a dusky area on the underside of the outer wing is distinctive in flight. First-winter birds also show a dark trailing edge and tail band, and a dusky bar across the inner-wing.

A bold and opportunistic feeder, the Black-headed Gull can often be seen following the plough with other gulls, taking advantage of exposed invertebrate larvae. They also feed on plant material, and fish, as well as scavenge. They are colonial breeders and also form flocks at other times. As well as reducing an individual's chance of predation, flocking behaviour allows the exploitation of abundant food sources and may have a role in transferring information between individuals.

WHERE TO SEE

Breeds around lochs and mires, on wet moorland and along flat coastline. Migrant flocks often follow the plough in spring and favour recently cut silage fields in autumn.

Common Gull *(Peerie Maa, Pikka Maa)*

Common breeding summer resident, migrant and winter visitor.

Adults separated from the smaller, slimmer Kittiwake by yellowish-green legs and the obvious white mirrors (spots) in the black wing tips. More gentle expression than larger Herring Gull, from which it also differs in adult plumage by dark eye, wholly yellow bill, yellowish-green legs and slightly darker grey upperparts. Juveniles have a neat blackish tail band, pale-fringed brown upperparts and wings, dark markings on breast and flanks, and dark bills. The mantle becomes grey and the bill develops a pale base during the first winter. Winter adults and second-year birds show an indistinct dark band on the bill and fine head streaking.

Despite its name, this is not the common gull over much of Britain. It is, however, common in Shetland. Our breeding birds leave in winter – one ringed on Whalsay wintered on the coast of Liverpool for four successive years in the 1980s – and are replaced by wintering birds from Iceland and Fennoscandia. Despite their rather genteel appearance, Common Gulls can be very aggressive in pursuit of food. They can often be found amongst flocks of Golden Plovers and Lapwings, where they soon give chase when a plover hauls up a worm.

WHERE TO SEE

The most common gull in built up areas. It breeds on the coast, on rocky hillsides and in towns. In winter it can be seen anywhere, forming large flocks on coastal headlands in severe weather.

Herring Gull *(Maa, Herring Maa)*

Common breeding resident and abundant winter visitor.

Herring Gulls are very similar in immature plumage to Lesser Black-backed Gulls. By their second winter (above) adult feathers show on the mantle and these are a distinctly darker slate-grey in Lesser Black-backs. Adult Herring Gulls have medium-grey mantles and pink legs, while Lesser Black-backs have darker slate-grey mantles and yellow legs. Both species show heavy head streaking in winter plumage

The Herring Gull was the subject of one of the classic studies into animal behaviour, when Nikko Tinbergen illustrated the role of the red spot on the lower mandible of adults. He was able to show that chicks have a powerful, innate tendency to peck at this red spot in order to get their parents to feed them. The breeding population of Herring Gulls in Shetland is in decline. A higher proportion of birds now breed in urban areas, often on roof tops, where the food supply is more predictable.

WHERE TO SEE
Breeds on rocky hillsides and in coastal areas. Migrants join other gulls on short, damp grassland and will often follow the plough in spring.

Lesser Black-backed Gull *(Swaabie, Swartback)*

Common breeding summer resident and migrant.

Differs from larger Great Black-backed by much smaller size, longer wings and thinner bill. Adult Lesser has slate grey upperparts and wings, which contrast with the black primary tips, and yellow legs. Greats show blacker upperparts and wings, contrasting little with the black primary tips, and pink legs. They also have massive bills. Juvenile and immature Greats tend to look whiter-headed than either Lesser Black-backed or Herring Gull.

The taxonomy of large, white-headed gulls remains challenging, as does their identification. It was once believed that Herring and Lesser Black-backed Gulls were part of a 'ring species'. As Herring Gulls expanded westwards from the Arctic Ocean their mantles became darker to become what we now know as Lesser Black-backed Gulls; those spreading eastwards, however, showed paler grey mantles. Eventually the pale-mantled American populations of Herring Gull crossed the Atlantic where they came into contact with the dark-mantled Lesser Black-backed Gull, the two now behaving as separate species. Since then, things have progressed a long way and the advent of DNA analysis has shown the ring-species concept does not apply to these large gulls, it is far more complicated than that. There is still disagreement, though, on exactly how many subspecies of Lesser Black-backed Gull should be recognised.

WHERE TO SEE

Breeds on moorland and along the coast. In winter can be seen anywhere and forms large flocks on coastal headlands in severe weather.

Great Black-backed Gull
(Swaabie, Swartback)

Common breeding resident and winter visitor.

This species is well known as a voracious predator, especially of ducklings and seabirds. Like most gulls, its jaw will unhinge to allow it to take larger prey whole. In common with many birds that live in marine habitats, gulls can excrete salt water from their nasal glands, although this is costly in energy terms. The excreted water has twice the concentration of salt in seawater, leaving a similar amount of salt-free water in the body.

The largest of the common gulls in Shetland. Heavy bill, pink legs and black upperparts, contrasting little with black primary tips, make adults distinctive. Immatures often lack black feathers on their mantle and back until their third year, and can be difficult to separate from immatures of other large gull species, although they always show a heavier bill.

J F M A M J J A S O N D

WHEN TO SEE

WHERE TO SEE

The harbours at Lerwick, Scalloway and Symbister (Whalsay) are good places to look, and individuals often join large flocks of roosting gulls on coastal headlands or freshwater lochs.

Glaucous Gull

Scarce migrant and winter visitor

Glaucous and Iceland Gulls share similar plumages which differ from other large gull species in having pale wing tips. Juveniles and first-year birds vary from very pale cream to biscuit brown in colour. The amount of pale grey adult-type feathers increases from the third year onwards. Adults are pale grey on the wings with a white trailing edge and wing tips. Iceland Gulls are smaller, slimmer and longer-winged than Glaucous, with rounder heads and thinner bills. In their first 12 months, Glaucous have a pink bill with a distinct black tip, whereas Iceland typically shows a darker bill with a varying amount of pale at the base.

The majority of records of this large Arctic gull in Shetland refer to birds in their first winter; young birds tend to move further south than adults in winter. The more experienced adults remain close to the breeding grounds so that they can quickly establish territories in the spring. Young birds will not breed for several years, so can afford to move further afield where living conditions are easier. On their breeding grounds, Glaucous Gulls often associate with predators like Arctic Foxes, being quick to exploit any eggs or chicks that are left unattended as a result of disturbance by the fox.

WHERE TO SEE

The harbours at Lerwick, Scalloway and Symbister are the best places to look, although can be found anywhere along the coast, or inland on short, damp grassland.

Iceland Gull

Scarce migrant and winter visitor.

A fail-safe way of separating Iceland from Glaucous Gull when perched, or on the sea, is to compare the length of the bill with the length of the primaries that project beyond the tail tip. In Iceland the primary projection beyond the tail is equal to, or greater than, the length of the bill, whereas in Glaucous it is usually distinctly shorter.

This species was added to the British List in 1822 by Shetland ornithologist Laurence Edmondston, who also recorded Britain's first Glaucous Gull. Its name is something of a misnomer as it does not breed in Iceland; most that occur in Shetland come from Greenland and north-west Canada. The numbers reaching Shetland are very variable but large influxes can occur, especially after long spells of north-westerly winds. No fewer than 400 were recorded in January 2012!

WHERE TO SEE

Breeds along the coast in crevices and caves. Seen widely around the islands, large flocks often gather on stubble in autumn.

Rock Dove *(Doo)*

Common breeding resident.

Essentially a pale grey pigeon with an obvious white rump and underwing in flight. The head and neck are iridescent and appear darker than the grey body. Two striking, bold black bars are obvious on the closed wing. In flight, grey with a narrow dark wing-bar, white rump and dark trailing edge to the wing and tail. Bill dark.

*The **Stock Dove** (inset) is a rare migrant in early spring and late autumn. It has a pale bill, is a darker grey, with two smaller dark marks on the closed wing and has a grey rump and underwing.*

This is the ancestor of the well-known Feral Pigeon, found in so many urban areas. True native Rock Doves still exist in the islands and breed in caves along the coast. They are monogamous and raise two squabs (chicks) per brood. Both parents care for the young, feeding them 'crop milk' – a pale yellow substance, high in protein and fat and with the consistency of cottage cheese. This is produced in the adult's crop a few days before the chicks hatch and regurgitated to them. Solid foods are introduced once the chicks are a week old.

WHERE TO SEE
Breeds in plantations
(e.g. Kergord) and gardens
with enough trees.
Migrants favour agricultural areas.

Wood Pigeon

Scarce breeding resident and common migrant

Having colonised Shetland recently, the population of Wood Pigeons is now increasing. Their nests, which comprise a simple platform of twigs in a tree, are not designed to cope with the Shetland climate and frequently get destroyed in strong winds. They are, however, capable of laying up to six replacement clutches in a season, although in Shetland they usually try just two or three times. Despite their size and bulk, Wood Pigeons can be surprisingly graceful when feeding, even hanging upside down to obtain seeds or berries.

Larger than Rock Dove. Adults differ from Rock Dove in having a yellow bill and eye, white neck patches and more uniform grey wings when perched. Juveniles have a greyer bill and lack the white neck patches but still look larger and more uniform than Rock Dove. In flight, appears heavier than Rock Dove, with distinct white wing patches and a grey rump.

WHERE TO SEE

Common in Lerwick and scattered around built up areas, especially where supplementary food is provided on a regular basis.

Collared Dove

Scarce breeding resident and migrant.

Smaller, more elongated and longer-tailed than our other common pigeons, with distinctly beige-brown plumage. The head is pale, and adults show a narrow, distinct black half-ring on the neck. Juveniles lack this neck-ring. In flight shows a darker outer wing and broad white tips to all but the central tail feathers. The bill is dark and the legs pinky-purple.

The first British record was not until 1955, part of a spectacular range expansion from Asia that occurred in the 20th century. It soon established itself as a common breeder in the UK, reached Shetland in 1960, and first bred here in 1965. The Collared Dove is one of the first species to start breeding in Shetland, with nest building sometimes beginning in January and young often fledging in May. The ability to raise up to six broods a year undoubtedly assisted its rapid westward expansion.

*The much rarer **Turtle Dove** is slightly smaller and has orange-brown edges to its dark-centred wing feathers and, in adults, a striped neck patch.*

116

| J | F | M | A | M | J | J | A | S | O | N | D |

WHEN TO SEE

WHERE TO SEE

Listen for calling birds in late spring.
Migrants can turn up anywhere.

Cuckoo *(Gok)*

Rare breeding summer visitor and scarce migrant.

Superficially like a hawk or falcon in flight due to size, long tail and pointed wings, but wingbeats very shallow, not really reaching above the body. Adults have a grey head, neck, breast, upperparts, wings and tail, contrasting with neatly barred whitish underparts. The yellow eye-ring can be obvious and the feet and bill-base are also yellow. Juveniles are heavily barred on their head and upperparts, which vary from greyish to brown, and on their whitish underparts.

The Cuckoo is a notorious cheat. Once the host has commenced laying her clutch, the Cuckoo lays an egg, which is very small in proportion to its body size, in the host's nest. Its incubation period has evolved to be very short, to ensure that the Cuckoo chick hatches before the eggs of its unfortunate host. The chick soon ejects these from the nest, leaving the confused parents to raise an imposter more than twice their size! In Shetland, the Meadow Pipit has been the host of choice. In recent years Cuckoos have become the focus of a well-publicised project, undertaken by the BTO, using satellite tags to track their annual migration to Africa.

WHERE TO SEE
*Migrants and winter visitors
often roost in conifers in
gardens or plantations.
Regular roosts form in some winters.*

Long-eared Owl

Scarce migrant and winter visitor. Has bred.

Long-eared and Short-eared owls tend to be found in different habitats: Long-eared usually roosts in trees and is rarely seen in daylight unless flushed; Short-eared roosts in long, grassy vegetation and often hunts before dusk. When perched, eye colour is a key feature – yellow in Short-eared and orange-red in Long-eared. The Long-eared also has longer, more prominent tufts (ears) although Short-eared can raise its ear-tufts a little too.

Long-eared Owls arrive in Shetland each autumn in variable numbers. Numbers follow a three to four year cycle, which is linked with the abundance of voles in Scandinavia. Females tend to outnumber males here by about four to one. Males prefer to remain on, or near, their breeding territories so that they can defend them or occupy them again quickly in the spring. Females have no such constraints, so are happy to move further afield where food supplies are more plentiful. In Shetland, mice, small birds and frogs form most of their diet.

WHERE TO SEE
*Favours areas of
rough grassland,
and often commences
hunting just before dusk.*

Short-eared Owl
Scarce migrant and rare winter visitor.

Although there is a good breeding population in Orkney, this species has never bred in Shetland, probably due to the lack of voles here. Like most predators, owls have forward-pointing eyes to give good binocular vision. Their ears are assymetric, each being a different size and each positioned at a different height on the head. This makes for better hearing, enabling them to pinpoint their prey more effectively. The flattened facial disk of an owl also funnels sound to the ears, magnifying it by as much as ten times. The wingbeats are silent to assist hunting.

In flight, Short-eared has longer wings with a more obvious pale, sandy patch in the primaries, shows a distinct white trailing edge to the wing and has a more strongly barred tail. Long-eared has shorter wings, a deeper orange primary patch and lacks an obvious white trailing edge. Heavy streaking is confined to the upper breast in Short-eared, whereas in Long-eared the streaking extends further down onto the belly.

J F M A M J J A S O N D

WHEN TO SEE

WHERE TO SEE

Most often seen at coastal
headlands or foraging
over large freshwater lochs
in poor weather.

Swift

Scarce migrant and summer visitor.

*Swifts spend almost their entire life on the wing,
where they feed on aerial plankton. Sleeping,
mating and feeding can all take place in the air and
they only land at the nest. The nest usually
comprises airborne material and feathers, glued
together with saliva. Their absence from the islands
as a breeding bird is probably due to an insufficient
quantity of insects. Each bolus of food presented to
the young contains an average of 300-500 insects
and spiders! Although Swifts are often confused
with swallows they are much more closely related
to hummingbirds!*

In Shetland only likely to be seen in flight, when
distinctive scythe-shaped wings, with rapid stiff-
winged wingbeats followed by long glides, should
enable identification. The plumage is dark
brownish-black with a paler throat. Larger than
Swallow – which it will often accompany when
feeding – with a different wing shape.

WHERE TO SEE
Best looked for at the usual migrant hotspots but can occur anywhere. Often feeds along tracks and minor roads.

Wryneck

Scarce migrant.

Larger than a sparrow with strongly cryptic, greyish-brown plumage. The upperparts are greyish with bold black marks through the eye, along the shoulders and running down the centre of the back. The underparts are buffish-white, finely-barred dark, and the tail is greyish with indistinct darker barring.

This cryptic species is a member of the woodpecker family. Like all woodpeckers it has two forward- and two backward-pointing toes and a stiff tail – both adaptations that help it to climb trees. Its ability to turn its head through more than 180° gives rise to its name, and when disturbed at its nesting hole, the adults and chicks will apparently sway their heads and occasionally dart their tongues out like a snake – enough to put any potential predator off!

WHERE TO SEE

Can turn up anywhere, although prefers trees if they are available.

Great Spotted Woodpecker

Scarce migrant, with occasional autumn influxes.

Unmistakable with black-and-white plumage and reddish vent, and behaviour; either perched on the side of a tree or fencepost, or hopping along the ground. Juveniles have a white forehead and red crown; adult males a white forehead, black crown and red on the nape; and adult females a white forehead with a black crown and nape.

This is an irruptive species and those occurring in Shetland are of the larger northern European race, rather than the smaller British race. In irruption years, upwards of 50 birds appear in the islands but in some years none are found. Irruptions are thought to occur when a food shortage, caused by failure of the pine and spruce crop, follows a successful breeding season. Less-experienced juvenile birds are forced to move considerable distances to obtain food, as they cannot compete with more experienced adults.

122

J F M A M J J A S O N D

WHEN TO SEE

WHERE TO SEE
Favours agricultural areas, where it often perches prominently on vegetation or fencelines.

Red-backed Shrike

Scarce migrant. Has bred.

Adult males distinctive with black mask, grey crown and nape, chestnut-red back, creamy underparts, grey rump, and black tail with white flashes at its base. In females (below right) the upperparts are generally reddish-brown, the underparts off-white, with varying amounts of fine barring, and the tail dark with a paler edge. The head can appear greyer and there is a hint of a mask. Juveniles (below left) are similar to females but also have barring on their upperparts.

Red-backed Shrikes feed on large insects, small birds, frogs and rodents. They often impale the corpses of their prey on the thorns of a bush or on barbed wire, to return to later – a habit which has earned them the nickname 'butcher bird'. This species was a relatively common breeder in Britain in the early 19th century but it has since undergone a spectacular decline and is now a very rare breeder. Climate change, the use of pesticides, intensification of agriculture and even egg collecting, may all be contributing factors.

The larger **Great Grey Shrike** (inset) is a rare visitor to Shetland in early spring and late autumn. Its black, grey and white plumage, very short wings and long tail are distinctive.

WHERE TO SEE

Agricultural areas. Often joins large flocks of crows or rooks

Jackdaw

Scarce migrant and winter visitor, with occasional large influxes. Bred in the 20th century.

Can be confused with other crows at a distance as it appears black, but is distinctly smaller and greyer-toned when seen well. The pale-grey rear crown and nape, and pale eye are diagnostic. Small size, more rapid wingbeats and smaller bill aid identification in flight. Its calls are higher-pitched than the other Shetland crows.

Males and females often mate for life and remain close together, even within flocks. Although flocks possess a hierarchical structure, with dominant and submissive individuals, pairs occupy the same place in this hierarchy. Unmated females are the lowest placed and have the last access to food and shelter. Jackdaws, like other crows, are attracted to shiny objects like jewellery, which they hoard in their nests.

Rook

Common breeding resident and scarce migrant.

Crow sized and shares black plumage of Carrion Crow. Adults best identified by greyish-white skin around base of bill and lack of feathers at nostril. Juveniles (above) decidedly more difficult as lack bare facial skin, but Rooks have a straighter upper mandible and a more pointed tip to the bill than Carrion Crow. Very challenging in flight, although Rook shows a more wedge-shaped tail.

J F M A M J J A S O N D

WHEN TO SEE

WHERE TO SEE

The main rookery is at Kergord, while the more productive agricultural valleys of Weisdale and Tingwall are the best places to look outside the breeding season.

Rooks nests colonially in rookeries, in which dominant birds occupy the centre, leaving less experienced individuals to breed at the edge. They are extremely sociable at other times of the year too, forming large flocks. Their diet consists predominantly of earthworms and insect larvae, although they will eat cultivated grain. Rooks are intelligent and, in captivity, will utilise tools. They have been shown to use stones to displace water if an earthworm is left in a part-flooded tube, and can even fashion wire into a hook to obtain food.

Hooded Crow
(Hoodie Craa)

Common breeding resident and scarce migrant.

Hooded and Carrion Crows are structurally identical. The Hooded Crow has a grey body, with a black head, breast, thighs, wings and tail.

J F M A M J J A S O N D
WHEN TO SEE

WHERE TO SEE
Found widely along the coastline and throughout crofting and hill land.

This was considered the same species as the Carrion Crow until recently, the two interbreeding freely and producing fertile offspring. The zone of hybridisation has remained narrow, though, lending support to the idea that the two do act as good biological species. One individual in Shetland clearly developed a taste for Fulmar eggs and could be seen repeatedly tugging at the wings of incubating Fulmars trying to force them to leave their egg – a risky strategy, given that Fulmar's need little encouragement to spit foul-smelling oil at intruders.

Structurally identical to Hooded Crow but plumage all black. Can be confused with Ravens and young Rooks.

WHERE TO SEE

Although more solitary than the Rook, they do occur in small flocks, particularly in spring in agricultural areas. They often accompany Hooded Crows and the two species have interbred in Shetland.

Carrion Crow

Scarce migrant and winter visitor.

Crows are highly adapted, intelligent and skilled animals. This is amply illustrated in Japan where they have learnt to drop nuts onto roads so that the oncoming traffic will crack them open. Some will even wait at pedestrian crossings until the traffic has stopped, before walking out to consume their quarry. It is their habit of taking the eggs and young of other birds, notably game birds, that has led to them being one of the most heavily persecuted species in Britain.

WHEN TO SEE

WHERE TO SEE

*Most breed on high sea-cliffs
but can be seen anywhere.
Non-breeders form
large flocks.*

Raven *(Corbie)*

Common breeding resident and scarce migrant.

Our largest crow. It has a distinctly heavier, thicker bill than Carrion Crow and may also show shaggy feathering on the throat. In flight it is longer-winged than other crows, with a distinctly diamond or wedge-shaped tail. The throaty 'prrrrk' call is diagnostic.

The large flocks of non-breeding Ravens seen in agricultural areas, or at the Lerwick landfill site, suggest that breeding territories are at a premium in Shetland. Breeding starts early, with the acrobatic aerial displays frequently seen during winter and nest building and egg laying commencing in February and early March respectively. Breeding success in Shetland is lower than in many areas of the UK and human persecution may be one factor contributing to this. The Raven is primarily a

scavenger in the islands, feeding on dead sheep and rabbits, but will also take seabirds and large insects. Surprisingly, the red seaweed *Corallina* has been shown to be prominent in the diet of some individuals. The Raven is the heaviest passerine (songbird), at around 1.2kg, and one of the longest lived, with some reaching their twenties. Ravens feature prominently in folklore and art, and in Shetland place-names, appearing as *Ramna* from the Old Norse word *rafn*, and as the Scots *Corbie*.

WHERE TO SEE

*Breeds in all but the wettest habitats.
Migrants can occur in
large flocks on brown earth in spring and
stubble in autumn.*

Skylark *(Laverek)*

Abundant breeding summer resident and migrant, scarce in winter.

Always feeds on the ground, where a combination of streaky brown upperparts, finely streaked, buff breast, unmarked white belly and often distinct crest, enables identification. Shows a pale eye-ring and supercilium, contrasting with brown ear coverts, when seen close. In flight the distinct white trailing edge and white sides to the tail, combined with the broad wings and dry, rolling call, enable identification. Its high, fluttering song flight is unmistakable.

Despite large declines over most of the UK, Skylarks are faring better in Shetland where agriculture is generally less intensive. Indeed, densities in the islands exceed those in much of the UK mainland and appear to be particularly high in some Great Skua colonies; perhaps the skuas offer added protection from predators. The male's hovering song-flight, which is such a feature of summer in Shetland, might have evolved as a means of illustrating fitness to potential partners.

Sand Martin

Scarce migrant.

Mostly seen in flight, when the sandy-brown
upperparts and well-marked brownish breast band
separate from the larger Swallow and House Martin.
Flight is rapid, with the wings held backwards
towards the body, and there is much less gliding
than in House Martin.

WHERE TO SEE

Can occur anywhere
but best looked for as it hawks
over nutrient-rich lochs in the
south mainland in April and May.

The Sand Martin is one of the earliest spring
migrants to appear in the UK. Males arrive at
the breeding colonies earlier than females and
start to excavate nests – tunnels in sandy banks,
up to a metre long. Despite their tiny feet, they
can excavate about ten centimetres a day!
Females often lay their eggs synchronously so
that the chicks hatch together, therefore all the
adults are out searching for food sources at the
same time. This is one of the migrants that
winters in the Sahel zone of Africa and numbers
in Britain can crash if a drought occurs there
in winter.

131

WHERE TO SEE

*Most breed in the more agricultural
areas of Shetland. Migrants can occur
anywhere but often gather to feed over
nutrient-rich lochs in poor weather.*

Swallow

Scarce breeding summer visitor and common migrant.

Spends much time on the wing, when the longish,
pointed wings and deeply forked tail, with long tail
streamers, give a characteristic shape. Adults have
glossy, blue-black upperparts, a deep reddish
forehead and throat, and a dark breast band,
contrasting with whitish underparts and under-tail.
Distinctive white spots can often be seen in the tail.

Juveniles show paler
throats, less glossy
upperparts and
much shorter tail
streamers.

*Shetland's breeding birds will often have two
broods in a summer and young from the first brood
may help rear the young from the second. The
male's long tail streamers are a result of sexual
selection. The longer his tail streamers, the more
attractive he is to a female; only a fit male (a better
potential parent) could carry such long tail
streamers and avoid predators. In the males of
some tropical bird species, sexual selection has led
to an amazing array of exaggerated feather tracts
and ornamentation that would appear to be a real
hindrance to survival.*

WHERE TO SEE

Migrants can occur anywhere but in spring they often gather to feed over nutrient-rich lochs in poor weather.

House Martin

Very rare breeding summer visitor and common migrant.

House Martins are monogamous, yet a recent study has shown that 15% of nestlings are not related to the male of the pair, while 32% of broods contain at least one chick that results from an extra-pair copulation. Although the male guards his female closely during courtship, his effort does sometimes slacken off after egg laying begins, allowing other males an opportunity to copulate with her. Some recent breeding attempts in Shetland have been in caves, a habitat that the species would presumably have relied on before man-made structures were available.

Spends much time on the wing like the Swallow but easily separated by obvious white rump patch. The upperparts are blue-black, and the underparts, including the chin, whitish. The tail has a shallower fork than in Swallow. The flight is more fluttering and less confident than the Swallow, but it does glide more than that species.

Migrants can appear anywhere but breeding takes place in well-established plantations. Kergord is a regularly-used site.

Goldcrest

Scarce breeding resident and common migrant.

Tiny, with fine bill, and often very tame. The golden or yellow crest and its dark border is shared only by the much rarer Firecrest, although that species has a dark eye-stripe and pale supercilium. The Goldcrest has a very plain face with a staring dark eye, indistinct pale eye-ring and a tiny dark moustachial stripe. The upperparts are greenish and the underparts off-white. There are two wing-bars, the lower much broader, and the tertials have neat white tips. Often heard before it is seen.

This is Britain's smallest bird, weighing in at between 4.5 and 7 grams. Their thin, high-pitched contact call is repeated frequently. Despite their tiny size, some spend the winter in Shetland. Being so small makes them unattractive to predators but results in a high surface-area-to-volume ratio, meaning they lose heat faster than larger birds and therefore need to feed almost continuously during daylight hours. Small groups defend feeding territories in winter and in severe weather will roost in tight-knit groups to conserve energy. Males have a brighter orange crest than females, which is often held erect during courtship.

Yellow-browed Warbler

Scarce, but increasing, autumn migrant, very rare in spring.

Distinctive, tiny, short-tailed warbler, smaller than Chiffchaff, with a long, prominent whitish supercilium, dark eye-stripe, two pronounced pale whitish wing-bars and whitish tips to the tertials. The upperparts are moss green and the underparts clean white. The distinctive high-pitched 'tsuwee' call can be surprisingly loud. Always on the move.

This is a Siberian species with our closest breeding population occurring in the Ural Mountains of Russia. On some late autumn days, however, it is the most common leaf warbler in the islands! Weighing as little as 5 grams (the same as a 20p coin) some may travel in excess of 3,000 miles to get here, though their intended destination is south-east Asia. It seems likely that a proportion of juveniles have a genetic defect, undertaking their autumn migration in the opposite direction than intended – so – called 'reverse migration'.

WHERE TO SEE

*Prefers older,
deciduous planted areas
for breeding but migrants
can turn up anywhere.*

Chiffchaff

**Common migrant. Has bred occasionally
and a few have been seen in winter.**

*The Chiffchaff's name is onomatopoeic, referring to
the song that often betrays its presence in spring.
Gilbert White, of Selbourne fame, was the first to
separate it from the similar looking Willow Warbler
and he did so because of the difference in their songs.
Breeding males fiercely defend a small breeding
range, typically measuring about 20m x 20m, but
have a much larger feeding range. Many contribute
little else to the breeding effort but some occasionally
help feed the young.*

Telling Chiffchaffs and Willow Warblers apart is a challenge even for experienced observers. A correct identification is best made by considering a number of features. In Chiffchaff the eye and pale eye-ring are often more obvious because they are set in a weaker head pattern; there is typically less prominent yellow on the underparts; and they usually show darker legs and look darker-billed than Willow Warbler. Tail movements can help – Chiffchaffs constantly dip their tail, whereas Willow Warblers tend to hold theirs more still.

Chiffchaffs of the Siberian subspecies **tristis** (inset) occur in late autumn. These lack yellow and green tones, appearing greyish-brown and white, with dark bare-parts.

Willow Warbler shows a more striking head pattern than Chiffchaff with a stronger supercilium, as pronounced behind the eye as in front of the eye, and a more marked dark eye-stripe. Willow generally has a stronger yellow wash on the face, supercilium and underparts (although this is variable), and usually has pale legs. Structurally, Willow has a longer primary projection than Chiffchaff and their longer wings give them a more attenuated appearance. The date can be a useful guide: Willow Warbler is very rare in Shetland before mid-April and after mid-October.

Willow Warbler

A common migrant, with breeding attempts becoming more regular.

Willow Warblers are unique among British songbirds, undertaking a complete moult twice a year. This means they have a new set of feathers for each of their long migrations. Like many songbirds, the adults pick up the faecal sacks produced by the chicks and dispose of them away from the nest so as not to attract predators.

Wood Warbler

Scarce migrant.

The bright yellow supercilium, sides of face, chin, throat, and occasionally upper breast, contrast markedly with striking silky-white underparts. The upperparts are much brighter green than Willow Warbler with more contrasting dark-centred, silver-edged tertials. The primary projection is much longer than Willow Warbler. Beware of bright Willow Warblers.

J F M A M J J A S O N D

WHEN TO SEE

WHERE TO SEE

Favours areas of woodland or scrub but can be found in more open places.

The British breeding population has declined by 70% since 1970. By undertaking detailed chemical analysis of feathers, grown during winter in Africa but collected in Europe, scientists have been able to identify key wintering habitats for the species. It appears that, unlike many other trans-Saharan migrants, Wood Warblers rely on woodlands in winter as well as summer. The loss of woodland in their winter quarters is likely to be a factor in their decline.

WHERE TO SEE

*Migrants can appear anywhere
but in spring often sing
from wooded gardens
or plantations.*

Blackcap

Rare breeding summer visitor and common migrant.

Medium-sized, plain, greyish warbler with a
distinct black cap in the male, and brown cap in
the female and juveniles. The juvenile's cap
becomes blacker through its first autumn (inset).
The upperparts are generally darker than the
underparts and there is no white in the tail. Gives
a hard 'tack' call similar to Lesser Whitethroat,
and has a lovely chattering, flutey song.

*The Blackcap is closely related to the Garden Warbler
and each responds to the other's song, meaning their
territories rarely overlap. A growing number of
Blackcaps breeding in central Europe now move west
to winter in Britain, presumably due to the general
warming of the climate and, possibly, the provision of
winter food by householders. Others continue to take
the longer route to winter in the Mediterranean and
North Africa. If successful wintering in Britain
continues, it is likely that an even larger proportion
of the population will winter here.*

WHERE TO SEE

*Favours areas of scrub
and plantations
but can be found
almost anywhere.*

Garden Warbler

Common migrant.

The Garden Warbler is a stocky, medium-sized, plain warbler. It is uniform greyish-brown above with a greyish shawl, and whitish below with unmarked wings. The face is plain, the legs and bill greyish. There is no white in the tail.

The Garden Warbler's featureless, plain plumage belies its beautiful song. In the mating game, birds tend to rely on a bright, eye-catching plumage or intricate vocalisations, but rarely both. If you can advertise yourself with a lovely song it makes little sense to increase your risk of predation by having spectacular plumage as well. Conversely, notice how many stunningly beautiful birds have comparatively bland songs. In addition to the pre-migratory fat they gain, research has shown that Garden Warblers can lose up to 20% of their breast and leg muscle and 40% of their digestive tract when migrating to winter quarters in Africa, highlighting just how demanding migration can be.

WHERE TO SEE
*Favours areas with tall
vegetation and scrub but newly arrived
migrants often occur
along dykes.*

Barred Warbler

Scarce autumn migrant but very rare in spring.

The Barred Warbler is a large, bulky warbler sometimes reminiscent of a small shrike. The head and upperparts are a pale grey and the underparts a buffy white. Look for the pale tips to the greater and median coverts, which form indistinct wing-bars, pale edges to the tertials and, if views allow, the distinct dark chevrons on the under-tail coverts. In flight they show white in the tail.

This is a rare bird elsewhere in Britain where it prefers to skulk in dense vegetation making life difficult for a would-be observer. It occurs more commonly in Shetland, where the lack of cover can make it surprisingly visible and where it occasionally even bounds around in the open! This is the classic so-called 'reverse migrant'; all autumn records are of birds in their first-winter and the theory is that, instead of following their normal south-easterly migration route, a small percentage of juveniles possess a genetic defect that makes them migrate 180° in the wrong direction, many ending up in Shetland.

WHERE TO SEE

Favours areas with tall
vegetation and scrub
but migrants can
appear anywhere.

Lesser Whitethroat

Common migrant, which has bred on several occasions.

The two whitethroat species bear a superficial resemblance in that both show a strong contrast between a darker face and a white throat, an indistinct paler area above the eye and white in the tail. The Lesser Whitethroat is a small warbler with a greyish head, often darker around the ear coverts, greyish-brown upperparts, white underparts, uniform wings and black legs.

The Lesser Whitethroat complex, or super-species, is a topic of hot interest amongst birdwatchers at the moment, as ongoing research seeks to establish just how many species it comprises. Up to six forms are recognised at present, three of which reach Shetland. Unlike most of our common trans-Saharan migrants, Lesser Whitethroats head south-east, rather than south-west or south, during their autumn migration.

Whitethroat

Common migrant, which has bred on several occasions.

Larger and longer tailed than the Lesser Whitethroat, with browner upperparts, rufous in the wings and pink legs.

WHERE TO SEE
Favours areas with
tall vegetation
and scrub but migrants
can appear anywhere.

Whitethroats underwent a spectacular crash in the late 1960s, which was evident even in Shetland where the number of recorded migrants decreased. It transpired that drought conditions in their main wintering area – the Sahel zone of Africa – were responsible for the decline. The species subsequently recovered until a further drought occurred in the region in 1984 – the same one that gave rise to Live Aid. This boom-bust trend may be part of a long-term cycle.

Marsh Warbler

Rare migrant, mainly in late spring, which has occasionally remained to breed.

In spring, the song is perhaps the best feature to separate Marsh and Reed Warbler: Marsh being more varied and Reed more repetitive. In silent individuals, concentrate on the upperpart colour and structure. Marsh shows distinctly more uniform, olive-toned upperparts, whereas Reed always shows some warmth on the rump. Marsh is slightly longer winged and has a broader-based, slightly shorter bill. Marsh also shows more prominent pale edges to the tertials, paler primary tips and paler, straw-coloured legs. They are even more difficult in autumn. Then, Marsh often looks a paler, more beige-brown on the upperparts with creamy flanks, while Reed always shows distinct warm rufous tones, especially on the rump, and often a rich buff wash on the flanks. The call can be very helpful: Marsh tends to chack, whereas Reed churrs.

The Marsh Warbler is a master of mimicry. An average male incorporates the songs and calls of up to 75 other species into its own song! Most of these it learns in northern Europe in its first few weeks of life, or during its first winter in south-east Africa. Mimicry in songbirds is often linked to male fitness – females select males for breeding on the basis of the complexity of their song – but surprisingly this appears not to be the case in Marsh Warbler.

Reed Warbler

Scarce migrant.

Reed and Marsh Warblers differ from most other warblers in their combination of a rather flat forehead, thin, longish bill, uniform brownish upperparts and whitish underparts, indistinct pale supercilium, which only just reaches the eye, and rounded tail.

*The **Icterine Warbler** (inset) is a scarce visitor in late spring and early autumn. It is superficially similar to Marsh and Reed Warblers but the longish bill is broader at the base, the wings are longer, the upperparts are a greyish-green, some yellow is always present on the underparts, a prominent pale panel is usually apparent in the wing, and the legs are distinctly blue-grey.*

The plain, unstreaked Acrocephalus warblers (including amongst others, both Reed and Marsh Warblers) present some of the toughest identification challenges for keen birdwatchers. Separation often comes down to subtle differences in colour tone and structure. An assessment of the wing formula – the respective differences between the length of each primary, whether or not these are emarginated on their outer web and the length of the notches on their inner web, can even be necessary to identify the most difficult individuals.

WHERE TO SEE

*Favours ditches and burns,
especially with tall vegetation
like canary grass.
Rarely seen in trees.*

Sedge Warbler

Very rare breeding summer resident and scarce migrant.

A medium-sized warbler with a rounded tail. The distinct, long creamy-white supercilium contrasts with a darker, diffusely streaked crown and dark eye-stripe. The mantle and back are finely streaked brown but the rump is a distinctly warmer orangey-brown, often obvious in flight. Some individuals show a little spotting on the breast sides in autumn. The underparts are whitish, often with a warmer wash on the breast and flanks.

All long-distance migrants lay down fat reserves before undertaking their long flight south in autumn but few can match the Sedge Warbler. They love aphids, and where these occur in high concentrations, such as reed beds, the warblers can increase their body weight by 50% in ten days! Migrant Sedge Warblers hunt at dawn and dusk, when their insect prey is more sluggish. Occasionally warblers live a surprisingly long time; the oldest Sedge Warbler on record was 10 years old.

*The **Grasshopper Warbler,** (inset) a scarce migrant in Shetland, prefers to run along the ground rather than fly when disturbed. Its dark-streaked, olive upperparts, relatively bland face pattern, long, broad, rounded tail and bright pink legs will enable identification. Getting a good view, though, can be challenging.*

WHERE TO SEE

Often visits gardens where it feeds on berries, rosehips, or apples provided by the householder.

Waxwing

Scarce autumn migrant sometimes occurring in large numbers. Rare in winter and spring.

Starling sized with unmistakable erect crest, pinkish-grey plumage, black lores and throat, chestnut under-tail, and a black and yellow pattern on the wing tips and tail. The red waxy tips to the secondaries can usually be seen. The flight is Starling like, with a stocky body and pointed wings, and the call – a ringing bell-like trill – is very distinctive.

The name comes from the bright red, waxy tips to the secondary feathers, which are in fact the flattened ends of the feather shafts. This is the classic irruptive species in a Shetland context; hundreds occur here in good years but in poor years they can be few and far between. Waxwings don't really have a song, probably because they don't defend territories. Their diet is largely fruit, although young, growing chicks require protein so are fed insects. Although fruit is rich in sugar, it is deficient in other nutrients, so Waxwings need to eat a lot of it. They can become intoxicated through fermentation of these sugars!

WHERE TO SEE

*Favours coastal cliffs,
steep-sided, heather-clad banks
or burns in moorland areas,
gardens and plantations.*

Wren *(Robbie Cuddie, Sistie Moose)*

Common breeding resident and rare migrant.

Its brownish plumage, small size and very short tail, often held cocked, are very distinctive. The fine bill and strong head pattern could suggest a Chiffchaff but the structure and behaviour is very different.

Three subspecies of Wren occur in Shetland, two of which - the Fair Isle Wren and Shetland Wren - are endemic, meaning they are found nowhere else in the world. They are both larger than their mainland cousins, with a flatter song. Both like to use geos as amphitheatres, amplifying further the sound of their loud song, which lasts about seven seconds yet comprises 100 different notes! These subspecies have only been isolated since the last glaciation around 10,000 years ago, nowhere near long enough to have evolved into different species.

*Favours coastlines and crofting areas
but can be seen anywhere.*

Starling *(Stari)*

Common breeding resident, migrant and winter visitor.

*Large pre-roosting flocks of Starlings (murmurations)
all moving in unison, with each individual mirroring
the direction and speed of its nearest neighbour, have
become something of a tourist attraction on mainland
Britain in recent years, although the population there
is in decline. They are faring better in Shetland where,
some authorities argue, they belong to a different
subspecies, known as zetlandicus. Fair Isle's Starlings
have been the subject of an intensive study for 40
years, which is revealing some fascinating insights into
their life history. Once confined to Europe and Asia,
man has now introduced Starlings to all continents of
the World, except Antarctica.*

The plumage and shape, notably the longish pointed
bill, short tail and flocking behaviour, separate
Starlings from Blackbirds. In adults, the pale spots of
winter plumage wear away to reveal a magnificent
metallic green-and-violet sheen in summer. Breeding
males have a blue-grey base to the bill, females a
pinky-yellow base. Juveniles (inset) vary from a pale
beige-brown to a dark sooty-brown, but soon moult
into a more spotted adult type plumage. In flight, the
broad pointed wings and short tail are distinctive.

Ring Ouzel

Scarce migrant.

Longer winged and longer tailed than Blackbird, and in spring the white (brownish-white in females) crescent across the breast is distinctive. Some autumn individuals lack this crescent altogether and are best identified by the pale edges to the wing feathers, which produce a striking pale panel in the wing. Listen for its harsh, staccato, fast-repeated 'tchack' call as it flies off, very different to that of a Blackbird.

The Ring Ouzel is the mountain equivalent of the Blackbird. The reason for its marked decline in Britain is currently the subject of research, both on the breeding grounds and in wintering areas in north-west Africa. The species is much shyer than our other common thrushes, often using dykes, quarries and cliffs for cover, and may fly long distances when frightened.

WHERE TO SEE
Breeds anywhere with
sufficient cover.
Migrants occur in open areas
and in woodland.

Blackbird

Common breeding resident, migrant and winter visitor.

Longer tailed than Starling. Also hops more, with frequent pauses, and usually more solitary. The male is all black in spring with an orange bill and eye-ring. Females and young birds are browner, often with paler throats and indistinct mottling on the breast, and have duller yellowish or dark bills. Fledged juveniles have pale spots on the upperparts too.

The breeding population of Blackbirds in Shetland is undoubtedly increasing; presumably the recent upsurge in gardening in the islands has increased the available breeding habitat, though some pairs nest on cliffs. As with all songbirds, the young are atricial – they hatch with their eyes closed and with little or no down and cannot leave the nest. Conversely precocial chicks, such as waders and ducks, are ready to leave the nest as soon as they hatch - their eyes are open and they are covered with down.

WHERE TO SEE

Migrants occur anywhere.
They are more solitary than most
other thrushes but can form loose
aggregations where food is plentiful.

Song Thrush

Common migrant and scarce winter visitor which has bred on several occasions.

In a recent RSPB poll to find Britain's best songster, the Song Thrush came out on top. Its bold, loud song can occasionally be heard in the islands. The thrush has dozens of phrases to call upon and it appears to select one at random and then repeat it several times before moving on to the next one. It is perhaps no surprise, then, that British colonists introduced it into New Zealand to make them feel at home there. In the North Island, where much of the landscape has been fundamentally altered, it has become one of the most common birds.

Significantly larger than pipits but much smaller than Mistle Thrush. The upperparts are greyish-brown or brown; the underparts boldly spotted, with a creamy-yellowish wash on the breast and flanks. The head pattern is relatively bland, with a hint of a pale supercilium in front of the eye, relatively uniform ear coverts and a dark malar stripe. The high-pitched, clipped 'sip' call aids identification in flight.

J F M A M J J A S O N D
WHEN TO SEE

WHERE TO SEE
Usually seen in
short, grassy fields,
occasionally joining flocks
of other thrushes.

Mistle Thrush
Scarce migrant and rare winter visitor.

Distinctly larger and longer-tailed than other thrushes, although the Fieldfare approaches it in size. Also differs from Song Thrush by colder-toned brown upperparts, bold spotting on whiter underparts, and more pale fringes on the coverts and tertials. The head shows distinct pale and dark patches on the ear coverts. The powerful, undulating flight shows off the white underwings and extensive white in the outer tail. The rattling, machine-gun like call is distinctive.

Mistle Thrushes are well known for singing from the highest trees in their territory, starting as early as November. They will continue even in adverse weather and this gives rise to the alternative name of 'storm cock' in some parts of Britain. They are also renowned for aggressively defending their nests, driving off potential predators such as crows and Magpies. This behaviour may extend into winter too when an individual may become very protective of its favoured feeding tree, preventing other thrushes from visiting it.

153

J F M A M J J A S O N D

WHEN TO SEE

WHERE TO SEE

*Flocks can occur anywhere
and in late autumn
can often be seen in
roadside fields.*

Fieldfare

Common migrant and winter visitor. Has bred.

A large, long-tailed thrush with a grey head and
nape, warm brown back, grey rump and dark tail.
A slight supercilium is evident and the creamy-
yellowish chin, throat and breast are heavily spotted
darker, with these spots continuing down the flanks.
The whitish belly and vent are unmarked. In its
undulating flight, the grey rump, white underwings
and dark tail are obvious. The chattering
'shack-shack-shack' call is distinctive.

*Like many songbirds the Fieldfare's summer diet
comprises mainly insects, with berries and seeds
becoming more important in winter. Large flocks
occur in Shetland in late autumn once the
Scandinavian Rowan berries are depleted. Head
up, chest out, and usually all pointing in the same
direction, they are constantly
searching for food. The Fieldfare
has unusual breeding habits for a
thrush as it will nest in small,
loose colonies, presumably as
protection against predators.*

WHERE TO SEE
Flocks can occur anywhere
and in late autumn
can often be seen in
roadside fields.

Redwing
Very rare breeding summer visitor but common migrant and winter visitor.

Size of Song Thrush but the striking white supercilium and moustachial stripe, and rusty-red flank patches are very distinctive. The upperparts are brownish and the underparts whitish, with heavy streaking on the chin, throat, breast and flanks. The call is longer and thinner than Blackbird and very different to the short, clipped call of Song Thrush.

In October and November, large flocks of migrant Redwings can arrive in Shetland. Two subspecies are involved; the slightly larger, darker and more heavily marked Icelandic form and the smaller subspecies that breeds from Scandinavia eastwards. The numbers involved can be breathtaking; over 65,000 were logged on Fair Isle on the 14th October 1979. Redwings are nocturnal migrants and in autumn flocks will often rise up high and head south as dusk approaches. This migration continues overnight and it is not unusual to hear the long 'seeeep' call of Redwings flying overhead on a calm October evening.

Spotted Flycatcher

Common migrant.

A long-winged, slim bird that often sits rather upright on an exposed perch, to which it will return after fly-catching sorties. The upperparts are generally greyish with fine, dark streaking on the crown, and the underparts are off-white with indistinct streaking across the breast. Although the wing coverts and tertials often show prominent pale fringes, there are no white wing patches and white is also absent from the tail. The bill and legs are dark.

The Spotted Flycatcher's dashing, agile flight in pursuit of insect prey, more than makes up for its rather drab plumage. Even large insects, such as butterflies, moths, bees and wasps are taken. Many of these are not available until later in the spring, so the Spotted Flycatcher is one of the last trans-Saharan migrants to return to its breeding grounds. The British population has declined by 80% in the last 25 years; the reduction in insects in the British countryside is likely to be a contributing factor.

The **Red-breasted Flycatcher** (inset) is a scarce visitor to Shetland, usually in autumn. Although superficially similar to the two more common flycatchers, the combination of a pale eye-ring, clean underparts, very narrow white wing-bar (if present at all) and white sides to the base of the tail are distinctive. It often flicks its wings and cocks its tail.

WHERE TO SEE

Favours areas of scrub and trees but can appear almost anywhere.

Pied Flycatcher
Common migrant.

The black and white males are very distinctive. The individual illustrated is in its first summer as it has retained its (browner) juvenile flight feathers. Some males lack black altogether, resembling females, but still show the large white wing patch and tiny white patch on the forehead. Females and first-winter birds are best identified by the contrast between the brownish ear coverts and the white throat, white edges to the tertials and greater coverts, a small white wing patch and white in the outer tail feathers. Often cocks its tail and flicks a wing up.

Many British songbirds are monogamous over one breeding season but the Pied Flycatcher is a confirmed bigamist. Larger, more experienced males will mate with two females. Once the first has laid her eggs, he sets up another territory between 200 m and 3.5 km away to attract a second female. He then returns to his first female to help raise their chicks. Once they have fledged he may take up residence with his second female again. It appears that she is aware of the situation though, as she will often lay a smaller-than-normal clutch, that she can raise on her own.

WHERE TO SEE

*Migrants can appear almost anywhere
with cover, but often favour dykes when
in open areas. Winters anywhere with
sufficient cover especially gardens.*

Robin

***Common migrant, but scarce in winter. Has bred
several times in recent years.***

Very familiar with orange face and breast,
surrounded by grey. The upperparts are olive-
brown and the underparts whitish. The dark legs
appear thin and long. The stance is upright and
birds often hop along the ground, drooping their
wings and cocking their tails. Juveniles, a very
rare sight in Shetland, lack any orange, instead
being a spotted buff and brown.

*As with many small songbirds mortality in the first
year of life is high – 75% of Robins die before they are
one year old. In many songbird species just 5% of one
generation contributes to the next generation. It is
easy to see, then, why natural selection can be such a
powerful agent of change. The oldest Robin on record
was eight years of age. In spring, when a male Robin
has decided on his mate, he will strengthen the pair
bond by bringing her food. It's a different story in
winter, though, when males and females aggressively
defend their own territories, and even birds on
migration will defend feeding territories.*

WHERE TO SEE
*Favours ditches,
damp areas along
the base of walls,
and manure heaps.*

Bluethroat
Scarce migrant.

Robin sized but slightly slimmer. The combination of the spring male's cobalt-blue chin, throat and upper breast, punctuated with a red spot on the throat and bordered below by a reddish band, is distinctive. In other plumages look for the striking whitish supercilium, white moustachial stripe and whitish throat, with dark malar stripes and a dark spotted breast band. The upperparts are brownish and when spread the tail shows rusty-red corners.

A male Bluethroat in spring is a highly prized find for a British birder, and Shetland is arguably the best place in Britain to see one. Despite their frequent, rapid runs, accompanied by much tail cocking, the red tail flashes are only obvious in flight. The Siberian population has increased, possibly as a result of global warming, and the species has now spread across the Bering Strait to breed in Alaska.

WHERE TO SEE

Can turn up almost
anywhere but favours dykes
and areas of scrub
or trees.

Redstart

Common migrant.

Both the Redstart and Black Redstart are slim, Robin-sized chats. They share an upright stance and often quiver their striking rusty-red tails. Adult males are easily separated: Redstarts have a white forehead, slate-grey upperparts, black throat and bright orange underparts; Black-Redstarts sport sooty-grey upperparts and greyish-black underparts, often (but not always) with a striking white wing panel.

The Redstart is one of a number of species whose occurrence in Shetland is linked to the weather during the spring and autumn migration periods. Winds from an eastern quarter (especially the south-east) push migrants off course as they head between Scandinavia and continental Europe. Many get displaced across the North Sea, ending up in Shetland. Occasionally huge arrivals, known as 'falls', occur; on the 9th May 1970 Fair Isle was ablaze with Redstarts, with a total of 700 recorded!

WHEN TO SEE

WHERE TO SEE

Favours beaches, quarries, dykes and derelict buildings.

Black Redstart

Scarce migrant and rare winter visitor.

Female and young Redstarts and Black Redstarts can be more difficult to identify. Black Redstarts show clear grey tones to both the upper and underparts, whereas in Redstart the upperparts are browner and the underparts distinctly paler and creamier.

This is one species that is at home in some inner cities, where it favours industrial complexes, derelict areas and even national monuments. One pair even bred on-site when the Millennium Dome was under construction. Another pair occupied a moving crane in Lowestoft, the adults following it up and down the dock to feed their chicks! Presumably these environments have something in common with its more typical habitat – cliffs, and stony ground in mountains.

J F M A M J J A S O N D

WHEN TO SEE

WHERE TO SEE

*Open areas where it likes
to perch on fencelines.*

Whinchat

Common migrant.

A small, short-tailed chat with longish, dark legs. The prominent pale supercilium easily separates it from Stonechat in all plumages. The brownish upperparts and rump are streaked darker, and the underparts grade from a rich orange-buff on the breast to a whitish belly and vent. The dark tail has white corners at its base, which are usually revealed in its frequent, short flights. The primary projection is longer than in Stonechat.

All birds have a complete moult at least once a year in which they replace all of their feathers, some of which have become worn and damaged. Moulting, migrating and breeding are the most stressful periods in a bird's year. Resident species can take their time to moult but summer visitors have to fit in a long migration south after breeding. Some species, like the Whinchat, moult in late summer, after breeding but before their autumn migration. Other species wait to get to their winter quarters before they undertake their complete moult.

WHERE TO SEE

*Any open habitats,
where it will perch
up on fences,
low scrub or tall herbs.*

Stonechat

Scarce migrant and very rare breeding resident.

The adult male is distinctive with its black head, white half-collar and rich reddish-orange breast. Some individuals show an obvious white patch in the wing, and the rump can be pale but is typically mottled dark. Females look much plainer, with a brownish head, and lack the white half collar and wing patch. Young birds are similar to females but often show a pale chin and throat.

The Stonechat is one of the few insect-eating birds that remain in Britain all year round. This makes it very vulnerable to long, harsh winters, after which the breeding population can crash. Its ability to raise two or three broods each summer means it is well equipped to recover from such crashes. After a series of mild winters, from 1968-1972, the Scottish population peaked in the mid-1970s, and it is perhaps no coincidence that breeding occurred in Shetland annually from 1975-77.

WHERE TO SEE

Breeds along the coast, on moorland and around crofts, even heavily grazed ones. Nests in dykes, ruined buildings and holes in the ground.

Wheatear *(Stenshakker, Stinkle, Shakk)*

Common summer breeding visitor and migrant.

A large chat that rarely seeks cover. In all plumages shows distinctive white rump and white tail, with an inverted black T – a pattern shared only by the rarer wheatear species. Spring males have a black mask, white supercilium, slate grey upperparts, buff underparts and black wings. Females and young birds have a less striking head pattern, greyish-brown or brown upperparts, and dark brown wings. Fledged juveniles have spotted upperparts and underparts but these are soon moulted.

The Wheatear is probably the only songbird that breeds in North America and winters in sub-Saharan Africa. Those breeding in eastern Canada fly from Baffin Island, through Greenland and Iceland (some probably passing through Shetland), and on to Portugal, the Azores and then Africa. Miniature tracking devices have confirmed that some individuals fly over 18,000 miles, before returning to their breeding grounds again! The wing length of more northerly breeding populations can be 10% longer than those breeding in Shetland – these 'Greenland' birds are regular in the islands on migration.

WHERE TO SEE
Migrants can turn up anywhere but generally favour cover. Gardens are preferred in winter.

Dunnock

Common migrant, a few remaining to winter. Has bred.

Note the thin warbler-like bill and pinky-brown legs. The head and underparts are grey toned with extensive dark streaking on the flanks. The upperparts are a warm brown, neatly streaked darker. No white in the tail. Dunnocks are discrete, often remaining on the ground under dense cover. Migrants are more likely to be seen out in the open.

One 19th century vicar considered the Dunnock to be the perfect example of humility and preached its virtues to his parishioners, exhorting them to emulate its behaviour. It is somewhat ironic, then, that recent research has shown that, in the world of the Dunnock, extra-pair copulations are rife. This species has a complex mating system in which trios are quite common. These usually consist of one female mating with two males, although single males may mate with two or three females. Occasionally, up to three males and three females may all be mating with each other!

WHERE TO SEE

*Found in towns and
around crofting areas.
Forms large flocks in oat
and barley fields in autumn.*

House Sparrow

Common breeding resident.

With its sturdy body and stout conical bill the House Sparrow is familiar to most. The male has black lores, chin and throat, grey on the crown and sides of its face, and chestnut from the eye back to the nape. The brown upperparts are heavily streaked black, the underparts an unmarked grey, and there is a broad white wing-bar. Females and juveniles lack

the striking head pattern, instead showing a faint supercilium bordering a brownish-grey crown. Flight is direct with rapid whirring wingbeats.

This is the most widely distributed bird on the planet due to numerous introductions and its ability to adapt to man. House Sparrows are sociable creatures, breeding in close proximity and engaging in communal activities such as dust and water bathing, and even social singing. As the breeding season approaches, the increasing day length triggers the release of a hormone, which results in an enlargement of the male's sexual organs, and prompts him to call near the nest site. House Sparrows pair for life, a trait that is unusual in a small songbird. They are one of only a few species in which juveniles undergo a complete moult soon after they leave the nest. Although the population of House Sparrows is declining in urban areas across Europe, the species is doing well in Shetland.

Most records come from crofting areas and gardens.

Tree Sparrow

Scarce migrant and very rare breeding bird.

Slightly smaller and slimmer than the House Sparrow, and easily told from that species by the combination of a wholly chestnut-brown crown and a prominent black cheek spot set in a white face. The sexes are alike.

The Four Pest Campaign was part of China's Great Leap Forward in the late 1950s. The grain-eating Tree Sparrow was identified as one of the four pests to be eradicated and three million people were mobilised to complete the task. As is so often the case, the impacts of so-called agricultural advances were not considered properly and nature's complex web began to unravel. Crop-eating insects, which also formed a large part of the sparrow's diet, increased dramatically in number, causing rice yields to slump, exacerbating a famine in which 20 million people starved. The Tree Sparrow was soon politically rehabilitated and the bed bug took its place as the fourth great pest!

J F M A M J J A S O N D
WHEN TO SEE

WHERE TO SEE
*Breeds in rocky,
fast-running burns,
otherwise found in wet ditches
and at manure heaps.*

Grey Wagtail

Very rare breeding summer visitor, scarce migrant and rare winter visitor.

Distinctly longer tailed than other wagtails, with black and white tail which is constantly pumped up and down. In all plumages, shows grey upperparts and a bright yellow vent. Breeding males have a narrow, white supercilium and white sub-moustachial stripe, contrasting with a black chin and throat, and yellow underparts. Females similar but with a less distinct face pattern, and first-winter birds show whitish underparts, often flushed with salmon-pink on the breast. The prominent white wing-bar is evident from above and below in flight, and the hard double 'tzip-tzip' call is distinctive.

Grey Wagtails love to bob, dash and duck along fast-flowing streams, constantly wagging their tail up and down as they go. This exaggerated tail movement may serve as a form of communication, telling other wagtails that a particular stretch of water is already occupied. Like some other songbird species, more southerly populations are resident but those breeding further north are forced to migrate when the weather deteriorates in late autumn.

WHERE TO SEE
*Breeds in banks and rocky slopes,
often near water. Migrants favour sandy
beaches with seaweed
and short, damp grassland.*

Pied Wagtail

Two subspecies occur: Pied Wagtail is a scarce breeding summer visitor and migrant; White Wagtail is a very rare breeding summer visitor but common migrant.

Essentially a black, grey and white wagtail. In breeding plumage male Pied (below) shows uniform black upperparts and male White (above) shows a sharp contrast between the black crown and nape, and the clean grey upperparts. This difference in upperpart colour holds for females too, although female Pied shows a more sooty-coloured mantle than the male. Juveniles (inset) can be very difficult to identify. Once they have moulted into first-winter plumage White shows a clean grey mantle and rump, and relatively clean white underparts whereas Pied shows a darker rump and darker grey flanks. In winter plumage both subspecies show a black breast band and have much reduced black on the head.

Up to 11 subspecies (or races) of White Wagtail are recognised, two of which occur in Shetland. Although some of these races are well differentiated, research into their taxonomy is ongoing. Gathering data on the races involved in breeding attempts in an area like Shetland can inform this research. If individuals of one race show a tendency to select mates from the same race, when both races are available, this suggests that they are acting as separate species.

WHERE TO SEE

Favours dry, longish vegetation and areas with bushes and trees.

Tree Pipit
Common migrant.

Very similar to Meadow Pipit and best identified by call – a more strident, incisive 'spizzz', as opposed to the Meadow Pipits feeble 'sip-sip'. Subtle plumage differences include the contrast between bold, heavy streaks on the breast and much finer, pencil-dash streaks on the flanks (the streaking is more uniform in Meadow) and a more striking black median covert bar with neat whitish tips. The legs are pink in Tree Pipit, more orange-toned in Meadow. Structurally slightly larger, with a stronger, broader-based bill than Meadow Pipit, and the flight is stronger and more purposeful. Tree often prefers longer vegetation.

Pipits spend much of their time walking around on the ground and have therefore evolved long hind claws. The Tree Pipit spends more time in scrub and trees than other British pipits and this presumably explains why its hind claw is shorter. In common with other British pipits, it too performs a parachuting display flight, but this starts from a tree or bush unlike that of the Meadow and Rock Pipit.

*The **Olive-backed Pipit** (inset), once a major rarity in Britain, is now expected in Shetland in late autumn. Its strong head pattern and lightly streaked, olive mantle are the key identification features.*

WHERE TO SEE

Breeds in open areas with enough vegetation to conceal a nest. Large flocks occur on migration, favouring short grassy areas for feeding.

Meadow Pipit *(Hill Sparrow, Teetik)*

Abundant breeding summer visitor and migrant, scarce in winter

Pipits are generally seen on the ground and show olive-brown upperparts with neat darker streaking, and creamy or white underparts with more distinct dark streaking. Their face pattern is indistinct, with a paler supercilium and sub-moustachial stripe, and a dark malar stripe. Two wing-bars are present but these can be relatively indistinct. The separation of Meadow Pipits from the other common pipits is discussed under the relevant species.

The Meadow Pipit is one of Shetland's most common breeding songbirds. It usually lays four or five eggs, which take around 11-15 days to hatch, and the chicks fledge about 10 to 14 days later. A pair may raise two broods over the summer. Pipits and wagtails migrate by day and, during the first half of September, in the right weather conditions, spectacular movements of Meadow Pipits can be observed at migration watch points like Sumburgh Head – a phenomenon known as visible migration. These occur in the first few hours of light, when hundreds fly south in loose flocks, some very low overhead.

WHERE TO SEE

Breeds along coastlines. Beaches with rotting seaweed and areas of damp grassland near the coast are favoured in winter.

Rock Pipit
(Banks Sparrow, Teetik)

Common breeding resident.

Slightly larger than Meadow and Tree Pipit but with a much less clean-cut appearance. The upperparts are darker olive or greyish-brown, with much less distinct dark streaking. The underparts are a dirtier white, with strong but more diffuse streaking. The supercilium is less obvious and the legs distinctly darker than in Meadow Pipit, and whereas Meadow and Tree Pipit show clean white in the outer tail feathers, Rock Pipit shows a greyish-white. Rock Pipit also has a longer and usually darker bill.

Until 1986 the Rock Pipit was considered to be the same species as the Water Pipit and the Buff-bellied Pipit; the latter two are rare vagrants to Shetland. Defining different species is not a precise science and can be controversial. Until relatively recently, relevant authorities made such decisions based on morphology and voice. Advances in DNA analysis, however, have allowed scientists to examine evolutionary relationships between different bird populations, and this has become a useful tool in assessing whether different populations are best treated as subspecies or separate species.

J F M A M J J A S O N D

WHEN TO SEE

WHERE TO SEE

Can occur anywhere but favours areas with scrub and trees.

Hawfinch
Scarce migrant.

A large, stocky, bull-necked and short-tailed finch, with pinkish-brown plumage. The huge, conical, pale bill makes confusion with any other finch unlikely. The black lores, pale greyish collar, white in the wing and tail, and glossy blue-black secondaries further aid identification. In flight, looks bulky with a broad white tip to the tail and a broad white wing patch.

Hawfinches are notoriously shy and retiring, and many birdwatchers get their best view of this species in Shetland, even though it is a scarce visitor here. Their huge bill is capable of generating enough pressure to crack cherry, olive and even plum stones. The Hawfinch's jaw muscles can exert a load of 30-48 kg – the equivalent of 60 tonnes for a human. Little wonder, then, that bird ringers are very careful when handling this species!

J F M A M J J A S O N D
WHEN TO SEE

WHERE TO SEE

Migrants can appear anywhere but often form flocks on stubble or turnip fields.

Brambling

Common migrant, with a few remaining to winter some years.

Similar in size and shape to Chaffinch but easily separated by its white rump and orange-tinged breast. Both sexes show an orange-buff wing-bar. Spring males have a black head and bill, orange throat and breast, and white underparts, but in autumn look much more like females, sharing their dark-sided, plain, brownish-grey face, boldly streaked buff upperparts, orange breast sides, dark-spotted rear flanks and dark-tipped yellowish bill. Like other finches, the tail shows a shallow fork in flight. The flight is strong and undulating like the Chaffinch, but the nasal call is quite different.

The Brambling moults in late summer, after which the male's mottled pale plumage is well adapted to provide camouflage as it forages on the forest floor. As spring comes, the pale-buff feather tips wear away and break off, revealing its striking black-and-gold breeding plumage. Bramblings are heavily dependent on beech mast and their wintering locations vary from year to year, depending on where the beech crop has been most successful.

174

WHERE TO SEE
*Breeds in well-wooded areas.
Migrants can appear anywhere
but often form flocks on stubble
or turnip fields.*

Chaffinch

Common migrant with a few remaining to winter. Has bred on several occasions.

The male is distinctive with its blue-grey crown and nape, deep pink face and underparts, double white wing-bar, reddish-brown mantle, greenish rump and white sides to the tail. The female shares the double white wing-bar and extensive white in the tail, but is greyish-green above and greyish-white below. Often forms mixed flocks with Brambling. The 'pink' call, given when perched, is distinctive, and the deeper 'tchup' call, given in flight, is quite different to Brambling.

The acquisition of song by young Chaffinches was the subject of an influential study by Cambridge ornithologist William Thorpe. He found that if a young Chaffinch is not exposed to the male's song during a critical period after hatching, it will never learn to sing properly. Since then, they have also been shown to sing with regional accents. Chaffinches feed their chicks on invertebrates, notably caterpillars, and breeding is timed to coincide with the availability of these. Unusually for a songbird, they typically raise only one brood a year.

Common Rosefinch

Scarce migrant

A nondescript sparrow-like bird. Juveniles have a very neat appearance; the dark eye is obvious, set in an otherwise bland face. The pale grey bill is conical but with a distinct curve on the upper mandible. The olive-brown upperparts are finely streaked darker and the whitish underparts show more heavy dark streaking. The two neat, pale wing-bars, and pale tertial edges are quite striking, and the wings (notably the primary projection) are much longer than in House Sparrow. Adult males show a rich red on the face, breast and rump. Note that the wing-bars can be much less evident on worn adults.

Males do not reach their reddish adult plumage until their second year. One-year-old brown males do sing, though, and will breed if the opportunity arises. The Common Rosefinch underwent a significant westward expansion during the 20th century and was widely predicted to colonise Britain, although this has yet to happen. In bird species, young males are often the pioneers in colonisation attempts; presumably it is easier for them to establish territories at the edge of the breeding range.

WHERE TO SEE

Favours gardens, plantations and tall vegetation with seed heads.

Bullfinch

Scarce irruptive migrant.

A distinctive, large, bull-necked finch with black face and crown, chunky black bill, ash-grey mantle, black wings and tail, white rump and whitish wing-bar. Males have bright pink underparts and females have greyish-buff underparts. The low-pitched, short, whistling 'piuu' call is distinctive.

Bullfinches arriving in Shetland belong to the northern race. They are more intensely coloured and 15% larger than their counterparts in mainland Britain. The numbers arriving in Shetland vary greatly but in autumn 2004 as many as 2,000 individuals reached the islands. Many of these had an unusual trumpeting call, suggesting they originated in eastern Russia. British birds are highly sedentary. The Bullfinch's bill is adapted for feeding on buds, and their passion for fruit trees has led to conflict with fruit growers on the mainland.

WHERE TO SEE
*Favours areas with
scrub or tree cover
and attracted to gardens
where food is provided.*

Greenfinch

Scarce migrant and winter visitor, several recent breeding attempts.

The British Greenfinch population has undergone a marked decline in recent years, due to a disease called Trichomonosis, caused by a protozoan that is spread in saliva. The disease is known historically from pigeons, but around 2006 it appeared to jump species and now effects finches. It is estimated that it has killed over half a million Greenfinches in the UK alone. On a more positive note, Greenfinches are well known for their remarkable display flight, when the male's wingbeats are so slow and deep that it resembles a butterfly.

A large, stoutly-built finch with greenish, or greenish-brown, and yellow plumage. Males show bright green bodies, with grey and yellow in the wings, grey sides to the face, and obvious yellow in the tail. In females and young birds the upperparts are a duller brownish-green with faint streaking, the underparts more greyish-toned, and there is less yellow in the wings and tail.

WHERE TO SEE

*Normally associated with
conifer plantations,
but in good years can be
seen anywhere.*

Crossbill

Irruptive migrant, common in some years, scarce or rare in others.

The bill of a Crossbill is unique, having crossed mandibles. Males are bright scarlet red and females a greyish-green colour. Juveniles are heavily streaked greyish-brown. The deep, hard, metallic call, repeated in series 'jip-jip-jip', often betrays their presence. Flocks of Crossbills usually feed unobtrusively in conifers, but in Shetland they will also take the seeds of thrift, thistles and oats, and even visit garden feeders.

The Crossbill's remarkable bill is well adapted to extract its main food source of pine and fir seeds. With its bill tip inside a conifer cone, the bird bites down, forcing the overlapping points of its bill in opposite directions, opening the cone and exposing the seed. The Crossbill is a highly irruptive species; in good years they raise multiple broods but if the cone crop fails, they are forced further afield in search of food. Over 1,000 have reached Shetland in large irruptions, but in other years numbers barely reach double figures.

WHERE TO SEE

*Most breeding attempts have been
in the south mainland and post-breeding
flocks often roost in the willows
at the Pool of Virkie.*

Linnet

Rare, but increasing, breeding summer visitor and scarce migrant.

The red forehead and breast, grey head and brown mantle, render a spring male unmistakable. Females and juveniles can be trickier, but a combination of the short, conical, grey bill, pale areas above and beneath the eye, streaking on the whitish throat, and brown mantle, should enable separation from the similar Twite. Although the flight call is similar to Twite it never makes the nasal call that gives Twite its name.

Linnets are often considered the southern counterpart of the Twite. There has been a widespread decline in the UK population due to the increasing use of herbicides, removal of scrub and over-zealous hedge trimming, but the species has recently colonised Shetland. Most finches feed their chicks at least some insects, as protein is required for chick growth and development, but Linnet chicks are fed exclusively on seeds. When the chicks are young, the male regurgitates food to the female, who in turn regurgitates it to the chicks.

WHERE TO SEE
*More coastal in summer
but flocks favour crofting areas,
especially grain crops and neaps,
in autumn and winter.*

Twite *(Lintie)*

Common breeding resident.

The Twite was formerly much more common in Shetland. Historically, local crofters killed many birds, regarding it as a pest, but a move away from traditional crofting to sheep grazing in the late 20th century is likely to have heightened its decline. This change has resulted in less acreage of the grain and root crops that harbour arable weeds, the seeds of which Twite are dependent upon in late autumn and winter.

A small finch, superficially similar to the Linnet, but longer tailed and can be separated by its unmarked buff throat and yellowish bill, although the latter is dark in the breeding season. Shows heavily streaked upper and underparts, and an indistinct buff wing-bar. Adult males show pink rumps. Its name is onomatopoeic, referring to its distinctive nasal 'chuwight' call.

WHERE TO SEE

Migrants can occur anywhere where
seed heads are present. Breeds in mixed
or coniferous plantations. Sandgarth,
has been a reliable site in recent years.

Common Redpoll

Rare, but increasing, breeding summer resident and common migrant.

A small finch. The red on the forehead, combined with the dark chin and lores, is diagnostic of redpolls, although the red is absent in recently-fledged juveniles. The upperparts are greyish to mid-brown, streaked darker, and the underparts off-white with heavily streaked flanks. The under-tail coverts, too, have dark feather centres. Adult males can have a rich reddish flush on the breast and occasionally the rump too. Common Redpolls often have pale rumps, but these are streaked darker. All redpolls have a hard, almost metallic, 'chutt-chutt-chutt,' flight call.

This species has a complex and controversial taxonomy. Three species are currently recognised – Lesser, Common and Arctic Redpoll – although all three have similar DNA and can look remarkably alike in the field. Redpolls are able to store food in an expandable part of their throat and digest it later. They are also adept at hanging upside down to obtain their food. Their plumage is very fluffy and their bodies are feathered in areas that other species are not – both adaptations to cold weather.

The rarer **Arctic Redpoll** (inset) usually has a large unmarked white rump and looks paler than its more common cousin.

WHERE TO SEE

*Migrant flocks can occur anywhere
and will visit gardens.
Mature mixed plantations, such as
Kergord, are favoured for breeding.*

Siskin

Rare breeding summer visitor and common migrant.

A small, short tailed finch with a long, pointed, conical bill. The plumage is essentially a combination of yellow, green, black and white. The pale patch at the base of the primaries, broad yellow wing-bar and yellow tail sides enable identification at any age. The male shows a black cap and chin, and an unstreaked yellow breast. The female has a streaked cap, while young birds are altogether more streaky and lack yellow on the underparts. The disyllabic 'pshu' flight call is very distinctive.

Siskins arrive in Shetland in variable numbers each year, probably related to the crop of birch and alder seeds on the breeding grounds in Scandinavia. They are social birds, breeding in loose colonies and occurring in flocks outside the breeding season. This is one of very few species in which subordinate birds within a group regurgitate food for more dominant members of the same sex. This may be a means of reducing aggression within the flock.

WHERE TO SEE

*Anywhere that suitable
seed heads for feeding occur.
Often attracted to garden feeders,
especially nyjer seeds.*

Goldfinch

Scarce migrant and winter visitor which first bred in 2013.

Adults are unmistakeable due to the combination of a red-and-white face, black cap and nape, gold in the wing, and black-and-white primaries and tail. Juveniles are much plainer, lacking the colour on the face, and have a streaked back and spotted breast, but still show the pattern of gold, black and white in the wings. The flight call is a distinctive twittering 'tirilit'.

The collective noun for Goldfinches is a 'charm', and with its beautiful plumage and song, it is easy to see why. It was among the most admired finches in the Victorian cage-bird trade and huge numbers were trapped. In 1860 it was alleged that 132,000 were taken annually near Worthing in Sussex. The population soon crashed in many parts of the country but has since recovered. The male has a slightly longer bill than the female, enabling him to reach further inside plants, such as teasel, for seeds.

WHERE TO SEE

Favours crofting areas with spilt grain, or weedy areas.

Yellowhammer
Scarce migrant.

Although a scarce visitor to Shetland, the Yellowhammer is the most widespread bunting in Europe. Most spend the winter close to their breeding grounds, but more northerly populations are migratory. It might not be Britain's most fluent songster but it is one of the most persistent and will sing throughout the summer. Some individuals repeat their song over 3000 times a day. Like many of Britain's seed-eating birds, its population has declined as farming has intensified.

A large, long-tailed bunting, usually with some yellow tones to the face and underparts, and a chestnut rump. The brownish mantle and dirty-yellowish underparts are streaked darker. Males can show reddish-brown on the breast. The face-pattern is typical of a bunting, with a pale supercilium and sub-moustachial stripe and dark-bordered ear coverts and a dark malar stripe. There is a distinct pale spot at the rear of the ear coverts. The flight calls comprise a hard 'tzit' and liquid 'pitilip'.

Any open area but favours the coast and stubble fields. Often occurs in large flocks.

Snow Bunting *(Snaa Ful)*

Common migrant and winter visitor.

Adult males are an unmistakable black and white. Females and young birds are potentially more confusing, although the large amount of white in the inner-wing and tail are distinctive in flight. Most encountered in Shetland show rusty-yellowish on the shoulder and cheek, a brownish crown, brownish upperparts, streaked darker, and a yellowish, conical bill. The musical, rippling flight call, interspersed with occasional ringing 'teu' calls, is distinctive.

Snow Buntings are said to be able to tolerate temperatures as low as -30° C. The male will feed the female while she is incubating so that she can remain on the eggs, keeping them warm. Historically, authors commented on how good Snow Buntings were to eat and they were a welcome supplementary food source to some Shetlanders in the 19th century. The number arriving in the islands may be linked to the North Atlantic Oscillation, a process that involves alternating periods of mild winters, with depressions situated over Iceland, and cold winters, with anticyclones over Iceland and Scandinavia.

*The **Lapland Bunting** (inset) is a scarce visitor, mostly in autumn, when it is best identified by a combination of a chestnut wing panel, two white wing-bars, relatively open face with dark spots at the upper and lower rear ear coverts, and a pale crown stripe. The dry rattling call is distinctive.*

Favours damp areas with longish, rough vegetation, and stubble fields.

Reed Bunting

Scarce migrant. Has bred.

In breeding plumage the male's black head and throat, broken only by a white moustache, is distinctive. The pattern remains the same in winter but the black is partly obscured by pale feather fringes. Females and immatures show a strong face pattern, streaked mantle, a chestnut area at the bend of the wing, and two buff wing-bars. The tail is often flicked out sideways revealing the white in the outer feathers. The typical call, a down-slurred 'siiuu', is distinctive.

Between 20 and 40 pairs of Reed Buntings bred in Shetland in the 1980s but the species is now extinct here as a breeding bird, and has also declined on mainland Britain. The Reed Bunting could arguably claim the ignominy of being Britain's most adulterous bird; recent studies have illustrated that around 70% of broods contain at least one chick that does not belong to the male of the pair, while in some nests, the male had fathered fewer than 50% of the chicks.

*The **Little Bunting** (inset) is a rare visitor, usually in late autumn. Its creamy eye-ring and warm chestnut ear coverts are good identification features. Like most rare buntings its call is a sharp 'tick'.*

Where to watch birds in Shetland

A selection of some of the most popular sites for birdwatching in Shetland is presented here. Access details are included along with, where relevant, the main species that can be found at each site. The approximate location of each site is marked on the map and a grid reference for each, is provided in the text. The relevant Ordnance Survey maps, Landranger 1-4, (1:50,000) or Explorer 466-470, (1:25,000) are recommended in order to follow the instructions.

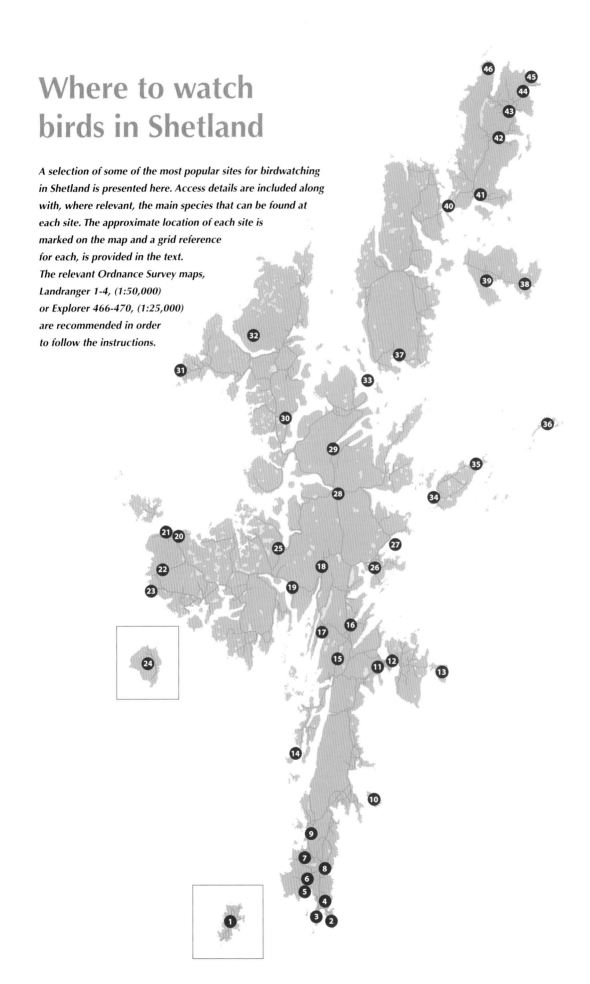

The view south towards Sheep Rock from the Fair Isle Bird Observatory.

1. **Fair Isle** (HZ2070):
Inter-island flight from Tingwall or ferry from Grutness.
Spring and Autumn: Internationally renowned Bird Observatory famed for its migrant birds.
Summer: Large and diverse seabird colony, with accessible Puffins, Arctic and Great Skuas, and one of only four gannetries in Shetland.

2. **Sumburgh Head** (HU4008):
Shetland Amenity Trust Visitor Centre and RSPB Reserve with parking.
Spring and autumn: Excellent site for migrants – check the roses to the south of the Lighthouse. The Sumburgh Hotel and the quarries and fields around the farm are all worth checking.
Summer: Very accessible seabird colony includes Puffins, Guillemots and Kittiwakes. Twite are often attracted to seed in front of the RSPB office.

3. **Scatness** (HU3809):
Park carefully at the end of the road so as not to block the turning circle.
Spring and autumn: The large, brackish Loch of Gards and adjacent marsh often hold scarcer species of duck such as Pintail, Shoveler and Gadwall. Walk out to the headland and check the wet pools and salt spray-washed turf for waders.
Summer: Arctic Terns often breed and attract Arctic Skuas. Kittiwakes may be seen collecting mud from the Loch of Gards.
Winter: Great Northern Divers and Long-tailed Ducks can be found in West Voe, Sumburgh and wildfowl occur on the Loch of Gards.

4. **Pool of Virkie** (HU3911):
Park in the turning circle at the willows (west end), or pull off onto the verge along the Pool. Low tide is best.
Spring and autumn: The best site in Shetland for waders. Look for scarce waders including Little Stints and Curlew Sandpipers in late August and early September.
Summer: Large flocks of terns gather here in late summer when wader migration is already under way.
Winter: Shelduck are present from January onwards along with wintering waders.

An aerial view of the southern tip of mainland Shetland. Sumburgh Head can be seen in the foreground and the Pool of Virkie is located behind the airport. The Loch of Spiggie is visible in the distance.

The town of Lerwick with the harbour in the foreground and the Lock of Clickimin behind.

5. **Quendale** (HU370131):

Park at Quendale Mill and walk west to the dam. *Spring and autumn:* Check the trees at the mill and the burn to the dam, for a variety of migrants. A good spot for Green Sandpiper and Jack Snipe.

Winter: Nearby Bay of Quendale has Great Northern Divers and Long-tailed Ducks.

6. **Loch of Hillwell** (HU373139):

Pull off along the road that runs south to Quendale and view with a telescope. Be very careful not to obstruct farm traffic. Do not walk down to the loch.

Spring and autumn: A good variety of wildfowl and waders is usually present. Terns and hirundines (Swallows and martins) often feed over the loch.

Winter: A good variety of wildfowl usually includes Whooper Swans.

7. **Loch of Spiggie** (HU3716):

View the loch and the marsh between here and the Loch of Brow from suitable pull-ins along the road. Park sensibly.

Spring and autumn: A good variety of wildfowl can be found including Whooper Swans in October and November. Terns, gulls and hirundines often feed over the loch.

Winter: The best place to see geese in Shetland. Glaucous Gulls often join the gull flock on the loch and Short-eared Owls sometimes winter in the marsh.

8. **Boddam/Voe** (HU399153):

View from the pull-in or turning circle on the north side of the voe. Park sensibly. Low tide is best.

Spring and autumn: Migrant waders.

Summer: Regular site for breeding Shelduck.

Winter: Wildfowl, waders (including Snipe and, occasionally, Jack Snipe) and Rock Pipits.

9. **Geosetter** (HU380201):

Park adjacent to the B9122 and walk up the stand of willows. Path and bridges provided.

Spring and autumn: A good variety of migrants can be found in favourable conditions.

10. **Mousa** (HU4623):

An RSPB Reserve. Boat leaves Leebitton daily from May to early September. Check times with The Mousa Boat.

Summer: Breeding Arctic Terns, skuas, Black Guillemots and waders. Special night trips organised for Storm Petrels.

11. **Loch of Clickimin, Lerwick** (HU463410):

View from the public road to the west of the loch. A footpath runs around the loch.

Spring and autumn: Wildfowl on the loch. Nearby bushes and gardens around the loch can hold migrants.

Winter: Goldeneye and Tufted Duck winter in good numbers, with the occasional rarer visitor. Gulls and waders can be found on the Clickimin sports pitches.

12. **Lerwick Harbour** (HU4742):

Access on foot along the waterfront and the fields and fish factories north of the town from Gremista Road.

Winter: Gulls and seaducks. The best place to look for Iceland and Glaucous Gulls.

13. **Noss** (HU5440):

A National Nature Reserve. Drive across Bressay to Noss car park. An inflatable ferry service operated by Scottish Natural Heritage runs across Noss Sound. Open from May to August, 1000 to 1700 daily (except Monday and Thursday) but best to check first with SNH. Tours by boat depart daily from Lerwick – check with the Tourist office.

Summer: Large and diverse seabird colony. Noss is one of only four gannetries in Shetland and Puffins are very approachable.

The plantations at Kergord House date back to 1913 and now offer some of the most diverse 'woodland' in the islands.

The west cliffs of Foula are the second highest in Britain at over 1200 feet. As well as providing a home for a diverse range of seabirds their height acts as a magnet for disoriented migrants.

14. **Minn Beach and Kettla Ness** (HU3529):

Park at the end of the road and walk around the coast.

Summer: Breeding seabirds including Arctic Skua, and waders.

15. **Lochs of Tingwall and Asta** (HU4142):

Drive along B9074 and view loch and adjacent fields from pull-ins and the boat shed. Park sensibly.

Spring, summer and autumn: Wildfowl, gulls and waders. Terns and hirundines often feed over the loch.

Winter: Check the Tufted Ducks for Scaup.

16. **Strand** (HU431460):

View from pull-ins along the B9074. Park sensibly.

Winter: A good site for Goosander. Nearby fields often hold geese, waders, Rooks and the occasional Jackdaw.

17. **Whiteness Voe** (HU3945):

View from pull-ins along roads that run along both the east and west side of the voe.

Winter: Great Northern Diver, Slavonian Grebe and Red-breasted Merganser are all regular.

18. **Kergord** (HU395541):

Informal access to plantations but do not enter gardens. The plantation surrounding Kergord House is often the most productive. Park sensibly in large pull-ins.

Spring and autumn: A reasonable variety of migrants can usually be found with a little effort.

Summer: Goldcrest, Siskin and Blackcap often breed. A Rookery is in the southern plantation near the farm.

19. **Tresta Voe** (HU3451):

Park in the large pull-in on the south side of the main road towards the east end of the voe.

Winter: Excellent site for Slavonian Grebe and Red-breasted Merganser.

20. **Loch of Collaster** (HU209572):

View from pull-in along minor road.

Winter: Wildfowl usually include Wigeon and Whooper Swan.

21. **Norby and Melby** (HU1957):

The area can be explored by parking either near the beach at Norby or the public toilets at Melby.

Spring and autumn: Terns, waders and wildfowl at the lochs and along the beaches. Migrant songbirds occur too.

Winter: The beach at Melby is usually a reliable site for Purple Sandpiper, with Long-tailed Duck and Great Northern Divers offshore.

22. **Dale of Walls** (HU179525):

Park by the crofts at the end of the road or near the cattle grid, but do not obstruct gates. A signposted footpath leads both north and south.

Spring and autumn: Check the buildings, bushes and burn for migrants.

23. **Watsness** (HU172500):

Park at the end of the road and walk down to the headland and look south.

Spring: Skuas pass offshore in north-westerly winds between mid-May and early June.

24. **Foula** (HT9738):

Inter-island flight from Tingwall or ferry from Walls.

Spring and autumn: Its remote location and height make it a magnet for disoriented migrants.

Summer: Large and diverse seabird colony includes one of the largest colonies of Great Skuas in the World. Red-throated Divers and waders.

The spectacular coastline of Eshaness can provide the first landfall for migrants from the north and west.

As Shetland's most easterly group of islands, Skerries is well situated to receive migrants when the wind is blowing from the east.

25. **Michaelswood, Aith** (HU340558):
   Car park at entrance. Woodland planted in memory of Michael Ferrie, with paths and benches.
   Spring and autumn: In common with most planted areas in Shetland this open woodland is attractive to migrant songbirds.

26. **Loch of Benston** (HU4653):
   View from pull-ins along the road that runs around the south and east side of the loch. Park sensibly.
   Winter: A good diversity of wildfowl usually includes Mute and Whooper Swans.

27. **South Nesting Bay** (HU4856):
   View from the many pull-ins along the road that borders the bay. Park sensibly.
   Summer: Seabirds can be seen feeding and seals, Otters and Harbour Porpoises can provide an unexpected bonus.
   Winter: Seaducks and divers are regular. A White-billed Diver has spent a number of winters at the north end of the bay.

28. **Voe** (HU413626):
   Park at the plantation by the Loch of Voe. The gardens of Lower Voe can also be productive but view only from the B9071.
   Spring and autumn: The sheltered location makes it attractive to migrants. The plantation is a good site for Crossbills in irruption years.
   Summer: Common Redpoll and Willow Warbler have bred in recent years and Common Sandpipers often occur on the loch shore.

29. **Sandgarth, Voe** (HU407683):
   Turn off the A968. A small parking area is available near the croft. The owners (Beth and Tony Gerrard) have turned the croft into something of a haven for wildlife and footpaths are provided. Be sure to inform them if you see something of interest.
   Spring and autumn: Migrant songbirds.

30. **Sullom plantation** (HU350727):
   Park sensibly along the road at the bottom of the plantation and follow the footpath.
   Spring and autumn: The cover attracts a variety of migrants.

31. **Eshaness** (HU2078):
   Park at the lighthouse and walk north or south.
   Spring and autumn: Superb scenery and geology. A few waders and pipits can usually be found, and migrant flocks of Snow Buntings occur in late autumn. Look for migrating seabirds offshore.

In Spring, Pomarine Skuas can be seen passing Watsness and Eshaness in suitable conditions.

32. **Ronas Hill** (HU335836):
   Park at the mast at Collafirth.
   Summer: Ronas Hill and the adjacent moorland and lochs of North Roe are home to a diverse assemblage of moorland breeding birds. Please dress sensibly as the weather can change quickly, and be prepared for a long walk.

33. **Yell Sound** (HU4577):
   The ferry between the mainland and Yell.
   Spring and summer: Seabirds feeding and flying to and from their breeding colonies, and the occasional sea mammal.
   Winter: Keep an eye out for Little Auks.

The picturesque village of Voe is positively sheltered by Shetland standards, allowing a good growth of trees that are attractive to migrant songbirds.

The Loch of Benston is one of the most important freshwater lochs for wildfowl in Shetland.

34. **Symbister, Whalsay** (HU5462):

Walk around the harbour. The marsh opposite the harbour and the gardens of Symbister are well worth a check but do not enter the gardens.

Spring and autumn: Migrants.

Winter: Gulls often include Iceland and Glaucous, and the Eider flock is always worth a check.

35. **Skaw, Whalsay** (HU5966):

Park sensibly near the end of the road. Check the croft gardens, dykes and crops at Skaw, and the golf course.

Spring and autumn: An excellent spot for migrant songbirds and waders.

36. **Skerries** (HU6871):

Ferry from Vidlin and Lerwick. Day-trips are possible on Friday, Saturday and Sunday but check the Shetland Islands Council ferry timetable.

Spring and autumn: One of Shetland's premier locations for migrants.

Summer: Breeding terns, a lovely day-out and always the chance of a cetacean from the ferry.

37. **Hamnavoe, Yell** (HU4880):

Take the B9081 from Ulsta. After about three miles park at the Hamnavoe Kirk. Look back west at the intertidal area. The nearby Loch of Galtagarth may have terns and wildfowl.

Spring and autumn: Migrant waders.

38. **Loch of Funzie, Fetlar** (HU653900):

A small car park is available at the north-west end of the loch, and a hide overlooks the mires to the south-east of the loch.

Summer: The best place to look for Red-necked Phalaropes but they are far from guaranteed. Red-throated Divers also present and Whimbrel often frequent the fields on the opposite side of the road. Check the willows by the hide for migrants.

39. **Tresta, Fetlar** (HU608904):

Park at beach and walk out onto the links. Check at the beach and Papil Water.

Spring and autumn: Gulls, terns, waders, wildfowl and the odd migrant songbird. Red-throated Divers are often on Papil Water.

40. **Bluemull Sound** (HU5599):

The ferry between Yell, Fetlar and Unst.

Summer: Seabirds flying to and from their breeding colonies.

Winter: Long-tailed Ducks, Eider and the occasional diver and Little Auk. One or two White-billed Divers winter in the area most years.

41. **Easter Loch, Unst** (HP599013):

View from pull-ins along the loch edge.

Spring and autumn: Wildfowl – a reliable site for Whooper Swans in late autumn. Be sure to check the surrounding fields and the Uyeasound beach for gulls and waders.

Winter: Wildfowl on the loch and seaducks and divers in the sound.

42. **Baltasound, Unst** (HP620087):

The houb at the head of the voe and the plantation at Halligarth (HP625093), to which there is public access, are always worth checking. Parking limited at both.

Spring and autumn: Waders on the houb and migrant songbirds at Halligarth.

Winter: Waders at the houb. The voe at Baltasound has become a regular site for Slavonian Grebes and a good number of geese frequent the surrounding fields.

43. **Haroldswick, Unst** (HP634120):

Park sensibly along the seafront. The bay, the pool behind the beach and associated scrub can be very productive.

Spring and autumn: A variety of migrants including waders and songbirds.

Winter: Great Northern Divers offshore, waders on the beach and wildfowl on the pool if the water levels are high enough.

The houb at Balta Sound is in the foreground. The sycamore plantation, established at Halligarth in the 19th century, is located in the middle of the photograph, its shape an indication of the prevailing wind direction.

Muckle Flugga, part of Hermaness National Nature Reserve, and the most northerly point of the UK.

44. *Norwick, Unst* (HP651145):

Park at the beach. The beach and the nearby fields and gardens are worth a look. Do not enter the gardens.

Spring and autumn: A good area for a variety of migrants.

45. *Skaw, Unst* (HP659163):

Park sensibly at the end of the road. Do not obstruct croft traffic and do not enter the garden.

Spring and autumn: Shetland's most northerly beach and the associated burn and croft are good places to look for migrants and boast an impressive list of rarities.

46. *Hermaness, Unst* (HP6115):

A National Nature Reserve. There is a car park at the reserve entrance.

Summer: Large and diverse seabird colony, including Shetland's largest Gannet colony. Skuas and waders on the moorland. Red-throated Divers often feed in nearby Burrafirth.

Common Gulls over breakers.

Useful websites

Fair Isle Bird Observatory: www.fairislebirdobs.co.uk
Nature in Shetland:
(for up-to-date news on wildlife in Shetland)   www.nature-shetland.co.uk
Promote Shetland: www.shetland.org
Rebecca Nason Photography & Design: www.rebeccanason.com
RSPB Shetland: www.rspb.org.uk/shetland
Shetland Amenity Trust: www.shetlandamenity.org
Shetland Biological Records Centre: www.shetlandbrc.co.uk
Shetland Bird Club: www.shetlandbirdclub.co.uk
Visit Scotland: www.visitscotland.com

Index of photographs

200

Photo credits

We wish to thank the photographers for providing additional images for the book and for permission to reproduce copyright material. Every effort has been made to acknowledge all photographers with their respective images and we would like to apologise for any errors or omissions should these occur. Please do inform us of any corrections that can be addressed in future editions of the book.
All images other than the ones credited below are by Rebecca Nason.

Gary Bell
P82, main; P146, main & top left.

Rob Fray
P160, top left.

David Gifford
P36, main; P41, main; P47, main; P123, top left; P135, main; P168, main; P192, bottom.

Phil Harris
P34, top left; P162, inset.

Paul Harvey
P149, top left.

John Laurie Irvine
P131, top left.

Jim Nicolson
P20, inset; P22, main; P41, inset; P47, main; P50, top left; P54, main; P58, top left; P64, top left; P73, main & top left; P82, top left; P83, top left; P102, top left; P103, top left; P123, bottom left & inset; P137, top left; P138, top left; P140, main; P143, top left; P144, top left; P145, main; P146, inset; P156, top left; P160, main; P176, top left; P184, inset.

Roger Riddington
P23, top left; P27, inset; P84, top left; P162, top left; P179, top left.

Richard Shucksmith
P6, main; P7, main; P8, top; P10, top; P46, top left; P100, main; P194, top & bottom; P196, bottom.

Paul Sterry/Nature Photographers Ltd.
P22, top left; P33, main; P42, top left; P46, main; P50, main; P53, main & top left; P55, top left; P57, main & top left; P58, main; P59, main & inset; P83, main; P85, inset; P86, main; P97, full page; P102, main; P127, main; P132, top left; P143, main; P144, main; P161, top left.

Roger Tidman/Nature Photographers Ltd.
P71, top left.

Rory Tallack
P38, top left; P116, main; P121, main; P133, top left; P137, main; P156, main; P170, main.

Brydon Thomason
P9, bottom right; P56, main; P72, main; P76, main; P81, bottom; P94, main; P99, main; P129, main; P139, top left; P145, inset.

Shetland checklist

Species on the official British List recorded in Shetland at the time of publication. Names and order follow the British List.

GUIDE TO STATUS
rare vagrant: <10 records
vagrant: less than annual
very rare migrant: almost annual but < 10 records a year
rare migrant: 10-20 records a year
scarce migrant: 21-200 records a year

Species	Scientific name	Status
Mute Swan	Cygnus olor	
Bewick's Swan	Cygnus columbianus	vagrant
Whooper Swan	Cygnus cygnus	
Bean Goose	Anser fabalis	rare migrant
Pink-footed Goose	Anser brachyrhynchus	
White-fronted Goose	Anser albifrons	scarce migrant
Greylag Goose	Anser anser	
Snow Goose	Anser caerulescens	vagrant
Greater Canada Goose	Branta canadensis	rare migrant
Barnacle Goose	Branta leucopsis	
Brent Goose	Branta bernicla	
Egyptian Goose	Alopochen aegyptiaca	rare vagrant
Shelduck	Tadorna tadorna	
Mandarin Duck	Aix galericulata	very rare migrant
Wigeon	Anas penelope	
American Wigeon	Anas americana	very rare migrant
Gadwall	Anas strepera	
Teal	Anas crecca	
Green-winged Teal	Anas carolinensis	very rare migrant
Mallard	Anas platyrhynchos	
Black Duck	Anas rubripes	rare vagrant
Pintail	Anas acuta	
Garganey	Anas querquedula	rare migrant
Blue-winged Teal	Anas discors	rare vagrant
Shoveler	Anas clypeata	
Pochard	Aythya ferina	
Ring-necked Duck	Aythya collaris	very rare migrant
Tufted Duck	Aythya fuligula	
Scaup	Aythya marila	
Lesser Scaup	Aythya affinis	rare vagrant
Eider	Somateria mollissima	
King Eider	Somateria spectabilis	very rare migrant
Steller's Eider	Polysticta stelleri	rare vagrant
Harlequin Duck	Histrionicus histrionicus	rare vagrant
Long-tailed Duck	Clangula hyemalis	
Common Scoter	Melanitta nigra	scarce migrant
Surf Scoter	Melanitta perspicillata	vagrant
Velvet Scoter	Melanitta fusca	rare migrant
Bufflehead	Bucephala albeola	rare vagrant
Goldeneye	Bucephala clangula	
Hooded Merganser	Lophodytes cucullatus	rare vagrant
Smew	Mergellus albellus	very rare migrant
Red-breasted Merganser	Mergus serrator	
Goosander	Mergus merganser	
Ruddy Duck	Oxyura jamaicensis	rare vagrant
Quail	Coturnis coturnix	very rare migrant
Red Grouse	Lagopus lagopus	
Red-throated Diver	Gavia stellata	
Black-throated Diver	Gavia arctica	very rare migrant
Pacific Diver	Gavia pacifica	rare vagrant
Great Northern Diver	Gavia immer	
White-billed Diver	Gavia adamsii	very rare migrant
Black-browed Albatross	Thalassarche melanophris	rare vagrant
Fulmar	Fulmarus glacialis	
Cory's Shearwater	Calonectris borealis	vagrant
Great Shearwater	Puffinus gravis	vagrant
Sooty Shearwater	Puffinus griseus	rare migrant
Manx Shearwater	Puffinus puffinus	rare migrant
Wilson's Petrel	Oceanites oceanicus	rare vagrant
Storm Petrel	Hydrobates pelagicus	
Leach's Petrel	Oceanodroma leucorhoa	very rare breeder and migrant
Swinhoe's Petrel	Oceanodroma monorhis	rare vagrant
Gannet	Morus bassanus	
Cormorant	Phalacrocorax carbo	
Shag	Phalocrocorax aristotelis	
Bittern	Botaurus stellaris	vagrant
Little Bittern	Ixobrychus minutus	rare vagrant
Night-heron	Nycticorax nycticorax	vagrant
Squacco Heron	Ardeola ralloides	rare vagrant
Cattle Egret	Bubulcus ibis	rare vagrant
Little Egret	Egretta garzetta	vagrant
Great White Egret	Ardea alba	vagrant
Grey Heron	Ardea cinerea	
Purple Heron	Ardea purpurea	rare vagrant
Black Stork	Ciconia nigra	rare vagrant
White Stork	Ciconia ciconia	rare vagrant
Glossy Ibis	Plegadis falcinellus	rare vagrant
Spoonbill	Platalea leucorodia	rare vagrant
Little Grebe	Tachybaptus ruficollis	
Great Crested Grebe	Podiceps cristatus	very rare migrant
Red-necked Grebe	Podiceps grisegena	vagrant
Slavonian Grebe	Podiceps auritus	
Black-necked Grebe	Podiceps nigricollis	rare vagrant
Honey Buzzard	Pernis apivorus	very rare migrant
Black Kite	Milvus migrans	rare vagrant
Red Kite	Milvus milvus	vagrant
White-tailed Eagle	Haliaeetus albicilla	vagrant
Marsh Harrier	Circus aeruginosus	very rare migrant
Hen Harrier	Circus cyaneus	rare migrant
Pallid Harrier	Circus macrourus	very rare migrant
Montagu's Harrier	Circus pygargus	rare vagrant
Goshawk	Accipiter gentilis	vagrant
Sparrowhawk	Accipiter nisus	
Buzzard	Buteo buteo	very rare migrant
Rough-legged Buzzard	Buteo lagopus	very rare migrant
Golden Eagle	Aquila chrysaetos	rare vagrant
Osprey	Pandion haliaetus	rare migrant
Water Rail	Rallus aquaticus	
Spotted Crake	Porzana porzana	very rare migrant has bred
Sora Rail	Porzana carolina	rare vagrant
Little Crake	Porzana parva	rare vagrant
Baillon's Crake	Porzana pusilla	rare vagrant
Corncrake	Crex crex	
Moorhen	Gallinula chloropus	
Coot	Fulica atra	
American Coot	Fulica americana	rare vagrant
Crane	Grus grus	very rare migrant
Sandhill Crane	Grus canadensis	rare vagrant
Little Bustard	Tetrax tetrax	rare vagrant

	Name	Scientific name	Status
☐	Great Bustard	*Otis tarda*	rare vagrant
☐	Stone-curlew	*Burhinus oedicnemus*	vagrant
☐	Avocet	*Recurvirostra avosetta*	vagrant
☐	Oystercatcher	*Haematopus ostralegus*	
☐	American Golden Plover	*Pluvialis dominica*	very rare migrant
☐	Pacific Golden Plover	*Pluvialis fulva*	rare vagrant
☐	Golden Plover	*Pluvialis apricaria*	
☐	Grey Plover	*Pluvialis squatarola*	rare migrant
☐	Lapwing	*Vanellus vanellus*	
☐	Little Ringed Plover	*Charadrius dubius*	vagrant
☐	Ringed Plover	*Charadrius hiaticula*	
☐	Killdeer	*Charadius vociferus*	rare vagrant
☐	Kentish Plover	*Charadrius alexandrinus*	rare vagrant
☐	Caspian Plover	*Charadrius asiaticus*	rare vagrant
☐	Dotterel	*Charadrius morinellus*	very rare migrant
☐	Upland Sandpiper	*Bartramia longicauda*	rare vagrant
☐	Hudsonian Whimbrel	*Numenius hudsonicus*	rare vagrant
☐	Whimbrel	*Numenius phaeopus*	
☐	Curlew	*Numenius arquata*	
☐	Black-tailed Godwit	*Limosa limosa*	
☐	Bar-tailed Godwit	*Limosa lapponica*	
☐	Turnstone	*Arenaria interpres*	
☐	Great Knot	*Calidris tenuirostris*	rare vagrant
☐	Knot	*Calidris canutus*	
☐	Ruff	*Calidris pugnax*	
☐	Sharp-tailed Sandpiper	*Calidris acuminata*	rare vagrant
☐	Broad-billed Sandpiper	*Calidris falcinellus*	rare vagrant
☐	Curlew Sandpiper	*Calidris ferruginea*	
☐	Stilt Sandpiper	*Calidris himantopus*	rare vagrant
☐	Red-necked Stint	*Calidris ruficollis*	rare vagrant
☐	Temminck's Stint	*Calidris temminckii*	vagrant
☐	Sanderling	*Calidris alba*	
☐	Dunlin	*Calidris alpina*	
☐	Purple Sandpiper	*Calidris maritima*	
☐	Baird's Sandpiper	*Calidris bairdii*	vagrant
☐	Little Stint	*Calidris minuta*	
☐	White-rumped Sandpiper	*Calidris fuscicollis*	vagrant
☐	Least Sandpiper	*Calidris minutilla*	rare vagrant
☐	Buff-breasted Sandpiper	*Calidris subruficollis*	very rare migrant
☐	Pectoral Sandpiper	*Calidris melanotos*	very rare migrant
☐	Western Sandpiper	*Calidris mauri*	rare vagrant
☐	Semipalmated Sandpiper	*Calidris pusilla*	rare vagrant
☐	Wilson's Phalarope	*Phalaropus tricolor*	rare vagrant
☐	Red-necked Phalarope	*Phalaropus lobatus*	
☐	Grey Phalarope	*Phalaropus fulicarius*	very rare migrant
☐	Terek Sandpiper	*Xenus cinereus*	rare vagrant
☐	Common Sandpiper	*Actitis hypoleucos*	
☐	Spotted Sandpiper	*Actitis macularius*	vagrant
☐	Green Sandpiper	*Tringa ochropus*	
☐	Solitary Sandpiper	*Tringa solitaria*	rare vagrant
☐	Spotted Redshank	*Tringa erythropus*	rare migrant
☐	Greater Yellowlegs	*Tringa melanoleuca*	rare vagrant
☐	Greenshank	*Tringa nebularia*	
☐	Lesser Yellowlegs	*Tringa flavipes*	rare vagrant
☐	Marsh Sandpiper	*Tringa stagnatilis*	rare vagrant
☐	Wood Sandpiper	*Tringa glareola*	rare migrant
☐	Redshank	*Tringa totanus*	
☐	Jack Snipe	*Lymnocryptes minimus*	
☐	Long-billed Dowitcher	*Limnodromus scolopaceus*	vagrant
☐	Woodcock	*Scolopax rusticola*	
☐	Snipe	*Gallinago gallinago*	

	Name	Scientific name	Status
☐	Great Snipe	*Gallinago media*	vagrant
☐	Collared Pratincole	*Glareola pratincola*	rare vagrant
☐	Black-winged Pratincole	*Glareola nordmanni*	rare vagrant
☐	Pomarine Skua	*Stercorarius pomarinus*	scarce migrant
☐	Arctic Skua	*Stercorarius parasiticus*	
☐	Long-tailed Skua	*Stercorarius longicaudus*	rare migrant
☐	Great Skua	*Stercorarius skua*	
☐	Puffin	*Fratercula arctica*	
☐	Black Guillemot	*Cepphus grylle*	
☐	Razorbill	*Alca torda*	
☐	Little Auk	*Alle alle*	
☐	Guillemot	*Uria aalge*	
☐	Brünnich's Guillemot	*Uria lomvia*	vagrant
☐	Bridled Tern	*Onychoprion anaethetus*	rare vagrant
☐	Little Tern	*Sternula albifrons*	rare vagrant
☐	Gull-billed Tern	*Gelochelidon nilotica*	rare vagrant
☐	Caspian Tern	*Hydroprogne caspia*	rare vagrant
☐	Black Tern	*Chlidonias niger*	vagrant
☐	White-winged Black Tern	*Chlidonias leucopterus*	rare vagrant
☐	Sandwich Tern	*Sterna sandvicensis*	
☐	Common Tern	*Sterna hirundo*	
☐	Roseate Tern	*Sterna dougallii*	vagrant
☐	Arctic Tern	*Sterna paradisaea*	
☐	Ivory Gull	*Pagophila eburnea*	vagrant
☐	Sabine's Gull	*Xema sabini*	vagrant
☐	Kittiwake	*Rissa tridactyla*	
☐	Bonaparte's Gull	*Chroicocephalus philadelphia*	rare vagrant
☐	Black-headed Gull	*Chroicocephalus ridibundus*	
☐	Little Gull	*Hydrocoloeus minutus*	rare migrant
☐	Ross's Gull	*Rhodostethia rosea*	vagrant
☐	Laughing Gull	*Larus atricilla*	vagrant
☐	Franklin's Gull	*Larus pipixcan*	rare vagrant
☐	Mediterranean Gull	*Larus melanocephalus*	vagrant
☐	Common Gull	*Larus canus*	
☐	Ring-billed Gull	*Larus delawarensis*	vagrant
☐	Lesser Black-backed Gull	*Larus fuscus*	
☐	Herring Gull	*Larus argentatus*	
☐	Yellow-legged Gull	*Larus michahellis*	rare vagrant
☐	Caspian Gull	*Larus cachinnans*	rare vagrant
☐	Iceland Gull	*Larus glaucoides*	
☐	Glaucous Gull	*Larus hyperboreus*	
☐	Great Black-backed Gull	*Larus marinus*	
☐	Pallas's Sandgrouse	*Syrrhaptes paradoxus*	rare vagrant
☐	Rock Dove	*Columba livia*	
☐	Stock Dove	*Columba oenas*	rare migrant
☐	Wood Pigeon	*Columba palumbus*	
☐	Collared Dove	*Streptopelia decaocto*	
☐	Turtle Dove	*Streptopelia turtur*	rare migrant
☐	Rufous Turtle Dove	*Streptopelia orientalis*	rare vagrant
☐	Cuckoo	*Cuculus canorus*	
☐	Black-billed Cuckoo	*Coccyzus erythrophthalmus*	rare vagrant
☐	Yellow-billed Cuckoo	*Coccyzus americanus*	rare vagrant
☐	Barn Owl	*Tyto alba*	vagrant
☐	Scops Owl	*Otus scops*	vagrant
☐	Snowy Owl	*Bubo scandiacus*	vagrant, has bred
☐	Hawk Owl	*Surnia ulula*	rare vagrant
☐	Long-eared Owl	*Asio otus*	
☐	Short-eared Owl	*Asio flammeus*	
☐	Tengmalm's Owl	*Aegolius funereus*	rare vagrant

	Common Name	Scientific Name	Status
☐	Nightjar	*Caprimulgus europaeus*	vagrant
☐	Needle-tailed Swift	*Hirundapus caudacutus*	rare vagrant
☐	Swift	*Apus apus*	
☐	Pallid Swift	*Apus pallidus*	rare vagrant
☐	Alpine Swift	*Apus melba*	vagrant
☐	Little Swift	*Apus affinis*	rare vagrant
☐	Hoopoe	*Upupa epops*	very rare migrant
☐	Blue-cheeked Bee-eater	*Merops superciliosus*	rare vagrant
☐	Bee-eater	*Merops apiaster*	vagrant
☐	Roller	*Coracias garrulus*	rare vagrant
☐	Kingfisher	*Alcedo atthis*	vagrant
☐	Wryneck	*Jynx torquilla*	
☐	Great Spotted Woodpecker	*Dendrocopos major*	
☐	Lesser Spotted Woodpecker	*Dendrocopus minor*	rare vagrant
☐	Lesser Kestrel	*Falco naumanni*	rare vagrant
☐	Kestrel	*Falco tinnunculus*	
☐	American Kestrel	*Falco sparverius*	rare vagrant
☐	Red-footed Falcon	*Falco vespertinus*	vagrant
☐	Merlin	*Falco columbarius*	
☐	Hobby	*Falco subbuteo*	very rare migrant
☐	Gyr Falcon	*Falco rusticolus*	vagrant
☐	Peregrine Falcon	*Falco peregrinus*	
☐	Red-eyed Vireo	*Vireo olivaceus*	rare vagrant
☐	Golden Oriole	*Oriolus oriolus*	very rare migrant
☐	Brown Shrike	*Lanius cristatus*	rare vagrant
☐	Isabelline Shrike	*Lanius isabellinus*	vagrant
☐	Red-backed Shrike	*Lanius collurio*	
☐	Lesser Grey Shrike	*Lanius minor*	vagrant
☐	Great Grey Shrike	*Lanius excubitor*	rare migrant
☐	Southern Grey Shrike	*Lanius meridonialis*	rare vagrant
☐	Woodchat Shrike	*Lanius senator*	vagrant
☐	Magpie	*Pica pica*	rare vagrant
☐	Jay	*Garrulus glandarius*	rare vagrant
☐	Nutcracker	*Nucifraga caryocatactes*	rare vagrant
☐	Jackdaw	*Corvus monedula*	
☐	Rook	*Corvus frugilegus*	
☐	Carrion Crow	*Corvus corone*	
☐	Hooded Crow	*Corvus cornix*	
☐	Raven	*Corvus corax*	
☐	Goldcrest	*Regulus regulus*	
☐	Firecrest	*Regulus ignicapillus*	vagrant
☐	Blue Tit	*Cyanistes caeruleus*	very rare migrant
☐	Great Tit	*Parus major*	very rare migrant
☐	Coal Tit	*Periparus ater*	vagrant
☐	Bearded Tit	*Panurus biarmicus*	rare vagrant
☐	Woodlark	*Lullula arborea*	vagrant
☐	Skylark	*Alauda arvensis*	
☐	Crested Lark	*Galerida cristata*	rare vagrant
☐	Shore Lark	*Eremophila alpestris*	very rare migrant
☐	Short-toed Lark	*Calandrella brachydactyla*	very rare migrant
☐	Bimaculated Lark	*Melanocorypha bimaculata*	rare vagrant
☐	Calandra Lark	*Melanocorypha calandra*	rare vagrant
☐	Sand Martin	*Riparia riparia*	
☐	Tree Swallow	*Tachycineta bicolor*	rare vagrant
☐	Swallow	*Hirundo rustica*	
☐	House Martin	*Delichon urbica*	
☐	Red-rumped Swallow	*Cecropis daurica*	very rare migrant
☐	Long-tailed Tit	*Aegithalos caudatus*	rare vagrant
☐	Greenish Warbler	*Phylloscopus trochiloides*	very rare migrant
☐	Arctic Warbler	*Phylloscopus borealis*	very rare migrant

	Common Name	Scientific Name	Status
☐	Pallas's Warbler	*Phylloscopus proregulus*	very rare migrant
☐	Yellow-browed Warbler	*Phylloscopus inornatus*	
☐	Hume's Warbler	*Phylloscopus humei*	vagrant
☐	Radde's Warbler	*Phylloscopus schwarzi*	vagrant
☐	Dusky Warbler	*Phylloscopus fuscatus*	very rare migrant
☐	Western Bonelli's Warbler	*Phylloscopus bonelli*	vagrant
☐	Eastern Bonelli's Warbler	*Phylloscopus orientalis*	rare vagrant
☐	Wood Warbler	*Phylloscopus sibilatrix*	
☐	Chiffchaff	*Phylloscopus collybita*	
☐	Iberian Chiffchaff	*Phylloscopus ibericus*	rare vagrant
☐	Willow Warbler	*Phylloscopus trochilus*	
☐	Blackcap	*Sylvia atricapilla*	
☐	Garden Warbler	*Sylvia borin*	
☐	Barred Warbler	*Sylvia nisoria*	
☐	Lesser Whitethroat	*Sylvia curruca*	
☐	Whitethroat	*Sylvia communis*	
☐	Dartford Warbler	*Sylvia undata*	rare vagrant
☐	Rüppell's Warbler	*Sylvia rueppelli*	rare vagrant
☐	Subalpine Warbler	*Sylvia cantillans*	very rare migrant
☐	Moltoni's Subalpine Warbler	*Sylvia subalpina*	rare vagrant
☐	Sardinian Warbler	*Sylvia melanocephala*	rare vagrant
☐	Pallas's Grasshopper Warbler	*Locustella certhiola*	vagrant
☐	Lanceolated Warbler	*Locustella lanceolata*	very rare migrant
☐	Grasshopper Warbler	*Locustella naevia*	scarce migrant
☐	River Warbler	*Locustella fluviatilis*	vagrant
☐	Savi's Warbler	*Locustella luscinioides*	vagrant
☐	Thick-billed Warbler	*Iduna aedon*	rare vagrant
☐	Booted Warbler	*Iduna caligata*	very rare migrant
☐	Syke's Warbler	*Iduna rama*	rare vagrant
☐	Eastern Olivaceous Warbler	*Iduna pallida*	rare vagrant
☐	Olive-tree Warbler	*Hippolais olivetorum*	rare vagrant
☐	Icterine Warbler	*Hippolais icterina*	scarce migrant
☐	Melodious Warbler	*Hippolais polyglotta*	vagrant
☐	Aquatic Warbler	*Acrocephalus paludicola*	vagrant
☐	Sedge Warbler	*Acrocephalus schoenobaenus*	
☐	Paddyfield Warbler	*Acrocephalus agricola*	vagrant
☐	Blyth's Reed Warbler	*Acrocephalus dumetorum*	very rare migrant
☐	Marsh Warbler	*Acrocephalus palustris*	
☐	Reed Warbler	*Acrocephalus scirpaceus*	
☐	Great Reed Warbler	*Acrocephalus arundinaceus*	vagrant
☐	Cedar Waxwing	*Bombycilla cedrorum*	rare vagrant
☐	Waxwing	*Bombycilla garrulus*	
☐	Treecreeper	*Certhia familiaris*	vagrant
☐	Wren	*Troglodytes troglodytes*	
☐	Starling	*Sturnus vulgaris*	
☐	Rose-coloured Starling	*Pastor roseus*	very rare migrant
☐	Dipper	*Cinclus cinclus*	very rare migrant
☐	White's Thrush	*Zoothera dauma*	vagrant
☐	Hermit Thrush	*Catharus guttatus*	rare vagrant
☐	Swainson's Thrush	*Catharus ustulatus*	vagrant
☐	Grey-cheeked Thrush	*Catharus minimus*	rare vagrant
☐	Veery	*Catharus fuscescens*	rare vagrant
☐	Siberian Thrush	*Geokichla sibirica*	rare vagrant
☐	Ring Ouzel	*Turdus torquatus*	
☐	Blackbird	*Turdus merula*	
☐	Eyebrowed Thrush	*Turdus obscurus*	rare vagrant
☐	Dusky Thrush	*Turdus eunomus*	rare vagrant
☐	Black-throated Thrush	*Turdus atrogularis*	vagrant

☐ Fieldfare	*Turdus pilaris*	
☐ Song Thrush	*Turdus philomelos*	
☐ Redwing	*Turdus iliacus*	
☐ Mistle Thrush	*Turdus viscivorus*	
☐ American Robin	*Turdus migratorius*	rare vagrant
☐ Brown Flycatcher	*Muscicapa dauurica*	rare vagrant
☐ Spotted Flycatcher	*Muscicapa striata*	
☐ Robin	*Erithacus rubecula*	
☐ Siberian Blue Robin	*Larvivora cyane*	rare vagrant
☐ Rufous-tailed Robin	*Larvivora sibilans*	rare vagrant
☐ Thrush Nightingale	*Luscinia luscinia*	very rare migrant
☐ Nightingale	*Luscinia megarhynchos*	very rare migrant
☐ Bluethroat	*Luscinia svecica*	
☐ Siberian Rubythroat	*Luscinia calliope*	rare vagrant
☐ Red-flanked Bluetail	*Tarsiger cyanurus*	very rare migrant
☐ Red-breasted Flycatcher	*Ficedula parva*	scarce migrant
☐ Taiga Flycatcher	*Ficedula albicilla*	rare vagrant
☐ Collared Flycatcher	*Ficedula albicollis*	vagrant
☐ Pied Flycatcher	*Ficedula hypoleuca*	
☐ Black Redstart	*Phoenicurus ochruros*	
☐ Redstart	*Phoenicurus phoenicurus*	
☐ Rock Thrush	*Monticola saxatilis*	rare vagrant
☐ Whinchat	*Saxicola rubetra*	
☐ Siberian Stonechat	*Saxicola maurus*	vagrant
☐ Stonechat	*Saxicola rubicola*	
☐ Wheatear	*Oenanthe oenanthe*	
☐ Isabelline Wheatear	*Oenanthe isabellina*	rare vagrant
☐ Desert Wheatear	*Oenanthe deserti*	rare vagrant
☐ Black-eared Wheatear	*Oenanthe hispanica*	rare vagrant
☐ Pied Wheatear	*Oenanthe pleschanka*	rare vagrant
☐ Alpine Accentor	*Prunella collaris*	rare vagrant
☐ Dunnock	*Prunella modularis*	
☐ House Sparrow	*Passer domesticus*	
☐ Tree Sparrow	*Passer montanus*	
☐ Yellow Wagtail	*Motacilla flava*	scarce migrant
☐ Citrine Wagtail	*Motacilla citreola*	very rare migrant
☐ Grey Wagtail	*Motacilla cinerea*	
☐ White Wagtail	*Motacilla alba*	
☐ Richard's Pipit	*Anthus richardi*	rare migrant
☐ Blyth's Pipit	*Anthus godlewskii*	rare vagrant
☐ Tawny Pipit	*Anthus campestris*	vagrant
☐ Olive-backed Pipit	*Anthus hodgsoni*	very rare migrant
☐ Tree Pipit	*Anthus trivialis*	
☐ Pechora Pipit	*Anthus gustavi*	very rare migrant
☐ Meadow Pipit	*Anthus pratensis*	
☐ Red-throated Pipit	*Anthus cervinus*	vagrant
☐ Rock Pipit	*Anthus petrosus*	
☐ Water Pipit	*Anthus spinoletta*	rare vagrant
☐ Buff-bellied Pipit	*Anthus rubescens*	vagrant
☐ Brambling	*Fringilla montifringilla*	
☐ Chaffinch	*Fringilla coelebs*	
☐ Hawfinch	*Coccothraustes coccothraustes*	
☐ Common Rosefinch	*Erythrina erythrina*	
☐ Pine Grosbeak	*Pinicola enucleator*	rare vagrant
☐ Bullfinch	*Pyrrhula pyrrhula*	
☐ Greenfinch	*Chloris chloris*	
☐ Linnet	*Linaria cannabina*	
☐ Twite	*Linaria flavirostris*	
☐ Lesser Redpoll	*Acanthis cabaret*	rare migrant
☐ Common Redpoll	*Acanthis flammea*	

☐ Arctic Redpoll	*Acanthis hornemanni*	very rare migrant
☐ Two-barred Crossbill	*Loxia leucoptera*	vagrant
☐ Crossbill	*Loxia curvirostra*	
☐ Parrot Crossbill	*Loxia pytopsittacus*	vagrant
☐ Goldfinch	*Carduelis carduelis*	
☐ Citril Finch	*Carduelis cirinella*	rare vagrant
☐ Serin	*Serinus serinus*	rare vagrant
☐ Siskin	*Spinus spinus*	
☐ Snow Bunting	*Plectrophenax nivalis*	
☐ Lapland Bunting	*Calcarius lapponicus*	scarce migrant
☐ Savannah Sparrow	*Passerculus sandwichensis*	rare vagrant
☐ Song Sparrow	*Melospiza melodia*	rare vagrant
☐ White-crowned Sparrow	*Zonotrichia leucophrys*	rare vagrant
☐ White-throated Sparrow	*Zonotrichia albicollis*	vagrant
☐ Dark-eyed Junco	*Junco hyemalis*	rare vagrant
☐ Black-faced Bunting	*Emberiza spodocephala*	rare vagrant
☐ Pine Bunting	*Emberiza leucocephalos*	vagrant
☐ Yellowhammer	*Emberiza citrinella*	
☐ Ortolan Bunting	*Emberiza hortulana*	very rare migrant
☐ Cretzschmar's Bunting	*Emberiza caesia*	rare vagrant
☐ Yellow-browed Bunting	*Emberiza chrysophrys*	rare vagrant
☐ Rustic Bunting	*Emberiza rustica*	very rare migrant
☐ Chestnut-eared Bunting	*Emberiza fucata*	rare vagrant
☐ Little Bunting	*Emberiza pusilla*	rare migrant
☐ Yellow-breasted Bunting	*Emberiza aureola*	vagrant
☐ Reed Bunting	*Emberiza schoeniclus*	
☐ Pallas's Reed Bunting	*Emberiza pallasi*	rare vagrant
☐ Black-headed Bunting	*Emberiza melanocephala*	vagrant
☐ Corn Bunting	*Emberiza calandra*	vagrant
☐ Bobolink	*Dolichonyx oryzivorus*	rare vagrant
☐ Brown-headed Cowbird	*Molothrus ater*	rare vagrant
☐ Baltimore Oriole	*Icterus galbula*	rare vagrant
☐ Ovenbird	*Seiurus aurocapillus*	rare vagrant
☐ Black-and-white Warbler	*Mniotilta varia*	rare vagrant
☐ Tennessee Warbler	*Oreothlypis peregrina*	rare vagrant
☐ Common Yellowthroat	*Geothlypis trichas*	rare vagrant
☐ Cape May Warbler	*Setophaga tigrina*	rare vagrant
☐ Magnolia Warbler	*Setophaga magnolia*	rare vagrant
☐ Blackburnian Warbler	*Setophaga fusca*	rare vagrant
☐ Yellow Warbler	*Setophaga petechia*	rare vagrant
☐ Chestnut-sided Warbler	*Setophaga pensylvanica*	rare vagrant
☐ Blackpoll Warbler	*Setophaga striata*	rare vagrant
☐ Yellow-rumped Warbler	*Setophaga coronata*	rare vagrant

In addition one further species has been recorded but as either/or:

☐ Fea's Petrel or **Zino's Petrel**	*Pterodroma feae/madeira*	rare vagrant

The following species may have occurred naturally in Shetland but are not currently included on the British List

☐ Ruddy Shelduck	*Tadorna ferruginea*	rare vagrant
☐ Wood Duck	*Aix sponsa*	rare vagrant
☐ Greater Flamingo	*Phoenicopterus ruber*	rare vagrant
☐ Saker Falcon	*Falco cherrug*	rare vagrant
☐ Daurian Starling	*Agropsar sturninus*	rare vagrant
☐ Chestnut Bunting	*Emberiza rutila*	rare vagrant
☐ Red-headed Bunting	*Emberiza bruniceps*	vagrant
☐ Yellow-headed Blackbird	*Xanthocephalus xanthocephalus*	rare vagrant